Dying to Belong

HOW I ACCIDENTALLY
FOUND MYSELF

Diane Mullins

Dying to Belong: How I Accidentally Found Myself
Published by Funshine Publishing
Cheyenne, WY

ISBN: 978-0-9974316-0-5

Personal Memoir

Cover and interior design by Victoria Wolf

QUANTITY PURCHASES: Schools, companies, professional groups, clubs, and other organizations may qualify for special terms when ordering quantities of this title. For information, email dimu524@msn.com.

This book is dedicated to my boys, Matthew and Hunter.
I love you both more than you will ever know. Thank you
for always inspiring me to be better. Please learn how to love and
respect yourselves and go get all you want out of life. Build
healthy, strong relationships everywhere you go
and make all your thoughts positive.

To my sister Lynn, who has loved me unconditionally
and taught me to be a better person, loves who I am, and helps me with
my relationship with God: thank you for always being there for me. To
my family, it's never too late to love and respect yourself. Thank you for
being a part of my life; you have all helped make me who I am today.

I also dedicate this book to my husband, Matt. This book
has been very healing and has made me discover the amazing person
I really am; thank you for allowing this to happen. I hope this book
helps you understand what I was going through in my mind while
recovering. I am very grateful I get another chance at life. May you
learn compassion and understanding from this book.

And I dedicate this book to ALL those who are stuck
and in their own way.

Stop holding back and go get it!

"One day... you will be at the place you always wanted to be."

~ANONYMOUS

Foreword

I MET DIANE MULLINS ABOUT nine years ago through our network marketing business. It was funny, because when I met her, she reminded me so much of myself: kinda crazy and didn't really think about what other people thought of her. We had just met, and we agreed to go to a convention and share a room for the next three days.

What a way to really find out about a person! I was very impressed with her, and what a hell of a body this woman had. There she was, training hard for a fitness competition at almost age fifty, yet she had the body of a twenty-year-old! I was so jealous of her! But throughout our time together, I began to see the real Diane. I don't think she realized her own true beauty, inside and out.

Here was a woman who had such a tough exterior, but was very fragile on the inside. Diane had been through a lot. As a child, she was sexually abused by a relative, and men had treated her terribly. I could see some deep-rooted issues that at the time, I'm not sure she could really see, let alone understand.

Diane is an incredible businesswoman. She took her business by storm, but something was still holding her back. It wasn't until she had a severe accident that she began to look deep inside. Imagine being at the top of your game, and your whole world stops. What would you do? Would you want to give up? Would you want to fight? Would you wonder why the hell this is happening to you? Those were the struggles that Diane felt. It was a time to go deep within.

Diane's story of redemption and perseverance is spellbinding. Her journey to recovery wasn't just about the physical healing, but also about the mental and psychological healing. It was a journey of going deep into the subconscious and finding out who she really was as a person. Why does she attract certain people or situations into her life? Did she create this accident through the power of her mind to thrust her into the reality of how she creates her life?

Diane understood that forgiveness is powerful, but mostly because it is about forgiving yourself and loving yourself! If you don't love yourself, how can you love anyone else? Here is such a beautiful woman, yet she didn't see her own beauty!

You will enjoy the ride as Diane transforms herself, and you'll understand that it starts with you. Her story shows the power of the subconscious. She began to see the belief systems and programs that were driving her, why she pushed people away from her that she loved and who loved her, and why she didn't love herself.

I am so excited as I've watched her through her journey. Some people would say, "You have blossomed into a beautiful flower." I believe she has morphed like a caterpillar into a butterfly. This isn't just a breakthrough in her life; this is her new life.

I know you will enjoy her journey as much as I have, and getting to know one of the most beautiful women whom I've ever had the privilege of calling my soul sister. Love ya, girl!

—**Deb Deaton**
International Best Selling Author of
Prison Without Bars
www.debdeatoninternational.com

The Accident

"Never throw away a chance to say, "I love you,"
to the people you care about because we
aren't promised tomorrow!"

—ANONYMOUS

"ARE YOU OK?" HE ASKED.

"No," I replied.

Holy shit! We just crashed

But there's no way; that can't be. I've never crashed before.
This can't be real; this cannot be happening. I lay there trying
to figure out what just happened, trying to assess both
the situation and my body. I wasn't sure yet if I could
even move; *nope, I couldn't.* As a former gymnast and
fitness competitor, I was very in tune with my body, so
I knew when something was out of whack and something was definitely not right. *Was I paralyzed? Could I*

move? I knew I couldn't breathe very well. I knew that I was in excruciating pain and that I had just been in an ATV accident. I knew that I was alive, literally alive, but severely broken.

Alive? What does that really mean? Literally speaking, alive and breathing. Figuratively, it means full of energy, spunky, and spirited. But I haven't always been alive, full of energy, or vivacious. That was something that definitely came later in life for me. As a kid, I just existed, no plans, no agenda, no goals; I functioned in survival mode most of my life. Very shy and introverted, I pretty much kept to myself, especially as a young child and adolescent.

Born in Iowa as the youngest of seven children, I never wanted to be the center of attention; I just wanted to exist. But I wanted to feel safe, secure, and loved. I was the fourth girl in the family, with three older brothers and three older sisters. This explains a lot about who I am. Or does it? According to most stereotypes, the youngest born is considered to be free-spirited, a risk taker, and spoiled. However, I didn't see myself as any of those. Shy, introverted, quiet, and very insecure—that was me. I didn't remember having any self-esteem or self-confidence EVER while I was growing up. I never knew what it was like to be in touch with my thoughts or feelings; I surely had no self-awareness.

I was raised in a Catholic family, a religion forced on us by our biological father, and I attended parochial school second through fifth grade. My grades and intelligence were far above average, even for private school. I always had to leave the classroom to go with a different group of kids. At the time I didn't understand what was really going on and why I had to leave my classroom; I just did as I was told. Later, I realized I was being put in advanced classes. Being smart and doing well in school were always important to me. I think now it was a subconscious effort to get attention from my family, to be good enough, to be loved and special. If I was smart, maybe I would be loved and find the security I so longed for. To this day if my intelligence is insulted, it drives me absolutely crazy; I hate it with a passion. For some strange reason, I felt the need to be intelligent in order to get love. It never got me the special attention as a child, and it certainly hasn't been beneficial as an adult in getting attention. But being smart is definitely important to me; it makes me proud of myself. So, I continued to challenge my intelligence and strive for straight A's as I acquired my master's in psychology.

In Catholic school guilt was instilled on a daily basis. I am not sure where it came from, whether it was how I perceived things to be or if it was actually pounded into me this way by the priest, nuns, and teachers. I just know guilt was a major influence in my life. If you don't do right, you will go to hell; if you don't do as you're told, you will go to hell; if you do bad things, you will go to hell; or even if you have bad thoughts, you will go to hell. I was so afraid to do wrong or be bad because of "hell," I stayed out of trouble. As a child, I don't think I really understood heaven or hell, but I was taught that hell was horrible, and it scared me enough to stay on the straight and narrow path.

I hardly ever got into trouble, wasn't mouthy, or ever had bad thoughts about anyone but myself. I wasn't perfect by any means, but I hardly ever rocked the boat. I do remember one time in school getting in trouble for laughing in choir. We had to kneel on a linoleum floor as punishment in the principal's office for about five minutes, which seemed like thirty at the time. It hurt our knees so much, I made a note to self not to laugh in choir anymore; I didn't like that pain at all. I was grateful it was for only a short period of time (although we have a very flawed idea of actual time).

Speaking of time, how long had I lain there, unable to move? I was face down on the hard, frozen gravel for what seemed like hours when I finally gathered enough energy to pick my head up. *Yup, I am alive. I am still breathing. I can move my head at least.* I was in shock that we crashed; I was numb. I have never crashed in all the six years I have owned those ATVs. I felt like everything around me just stopped for hours, waiting for me to move. I was not scared or angry, just numb mentally and physically. I was definitely in denial that we crashed and wasn't ready to accept that reality yet. *A crash? No way!*

I still could not wrap my head around that concept. I picked myself up onto my elbows at least, where I stayed for a minute, then tried to get up on my hands and knees, but my body hurt; I mean hurt beyond comprehension. You know that kind of hurt that puts you into a numb sort of state? Your thoughts are spinning looking for clarity and understanding. I knew something was terribly wrong, but my brain could not wrap the thoughts or feelings around what was really going on. I could not think of any words that described my state emotionally, mentally, and physically. I was in survival mode. I could move, but I was in so much pain, it was unbelievable. I have never been in that much pain before; it was almost paralyzing in every way.

I could barely get to my knees, but I managed miraculously. I had to get to my feet; crawling was way too painful. *What the hell is going on? I can't even hold myself up on my hands and knees. Wow! Things must be bad. Where am I crawling to? Where am I supposed to be going? What is going on here?* My body wasn't working right; it was functioning, but something was certainly wrong. I was confused, I was perplexed, I was speechless. My mind was boggled, and I still could not wrap my head around that crash. I was concerned that I wasn't going to be OK, but I reassured myself it was all going to be all right: *Don't panic; just stand up; it will all be OK if I can just stand. You got this, sister, you are strong; you are going to be OK.*

As a very active person, both as a child and adult, I've been in pain, pulled muscles, birthed children, and have had sore muscles, broken bones, bruises, and stitches. However, those past experiences did not hold a candle to what I experienced that day, to that level of pain. With significant struggle and with every ounce of strength I had, I finally got to my feet. I was moving in slow motion, but I was moving. Time didn't matter at that point since the world had stopped and waited for me to get moving again. I did it; I made it; I was on my feet. My body could barely stand upright, but it was standing. I felt like a drunk wavering back and forth trying to focus my eyes. I just stood with my feet planted on the parched, solid, frozen dirt still trying to get some clarity. I could not hear anything; I could not comprehend anything; I was in la-la land.

Suddenly I was snapped back to reality, with a man's voice in the background. I heard my boyfriend, Matt, say to his friend Chris, who was with us that day, "Go help her."

I wanted to turn my head, which was still encased by my helmet, toward that scared, rattled voice. I still couldn't see anything as I stood there, but I heard him speak. I had never heard his voice sound like that before, with such serious concern in his tone. As I tried to look around to see where they were, I realized I couldn't move my head very well. I continued the struggle to breathe. I battled so hard to grasp for air, like something was squeezing my chest or compressing my back making it impossible to inhale. Surely, I had just knocked the wind out of myself, which I have done many times before. Not being able to breathe was usually so scary for me, feeling claustrophobic and putting me into panic mode, making my heart beat faster and faster. Although that was a typical reaction for me, none of those reactions happened that day. I was pretty calm, composed, as I just listened to what my subconscious brain was telling me to do, which was walk toward the ATV and get the hell out of there. Fortunately, my subconscious went into survival mode and knew better than my conscious mind what I needed to do. I never once felt like I needed to panic. I knew I would be taken care of by someone, somewhere, somehow.

I was putting a lot of trust into someone or something that day, which was unusual for me. I don't trust easily, so to trust that day was amazing. I have been hurt, betrayed, and lied to so many times throughout my life by people who were supposed to take care of me and protect me that my trust has been shattered. It is fascinating that as infants we just trust that people are going to take care of us and that all our needs will be met. As children, we start to learn people are not always true to their word, and we start being disappointed. Our trust is challenged early on. Unfortunately, as life continues, we see more bad things and more wrongs being done to each other; it is a wonder there is any trust left. Can we learn to trust like an infant again? Who should we trust? Who shouldn't we trust? How do we know the difference? Trust is something I still battle with today.

Even though I still had no idea about the extent of my injuries, I knew that something was definitely broken. In the midst of all that rolling, tumbling, and banging around, I heard a loud, distinct cracking sound very close to my ear. I thought I had broken my jaw. But as I concentrated on my jaw for a second, opening and closing my mouth, moving my jaw from side to side, I realized it was fine. Although I was almost numb, I took a few minutes to figure out what hurt the most. I could not feel anything specific; I was in so much pain, my whole body hurt. Things were still foggy and confusing. You know how when someone is talking to you, you're there physically but not paying attention to what they are really saying? That's how I felt, I was present and hurting but couldn't pinpoint exactly how I felt.

During the tumbling, I felt something smack against my helmet a few times, and I recalled seeing dirt, sky, dirt, sky, so I knew I had rolled and banged my head. My head did not really hurt either. *Weird, this is so weird,* I kept thinking: *I have never experienced this pain and numbness simultaneously before.* I was brought back to reality with pain as I tried to inhale deeply. My back hurt so bad, mostly on the left side. The pain was excruciating. I took my right hand, reached around, got it under my coat and sweater, and touched my back. It felt like the left back side of my rib cage was sticking out about three inches farther than the right. Holy crap. I realized again something was horribly wrong; something was not normal. I didn't go into panic mode, although I thought for a second maybe I should freak out. I don't normally overreact to pain and am not the kind to rush to the doctor, and certainly didn't have a sense of urgency that day. I almost felt relieved when I discovered what hurt the most; I was making some headway on assessing my injuries.

I continued to move my hand around a little more to see if anything was poking out of my skin. Not finding anything protruding, I reassured myself that was a good thing. I confirmed by feeling the left side again just to make sure I felt it correctly the first time. *Yep, it is definitely out of whack.* Panic still barely crossed my mind. I resumed my assessment as the pain and lack of breathing intensified. *If I have knocked the wind out of myself, I should be back to normal soon.*

As a very active country kid, horse owner, and gymnast, Lord knows, I have had the wind knocked out of me before, many times in fact. It hurts for a second or two, it's hard to breathe, but it usually goes back to normal within a few minutes. I totally had lost track of time. I stood there for what seemed like hours trying to figure out what to do next. Even though I had not fully assessed my injuries, I knew Matt was also hurt, as I heard him talk to Chris about a bloody arm and mud on his face. I was not able to fully focus on the words being said due to the denial I was still in about the crash. I couldn't even begin to explain how I felt about the disaster. To say shocked, stunned, appalled, or perplexed would be an understatement.

Growing up with dirt bikes, horses, go-karts, and bicycles, I knew crashes were part of the deal, and we definitely had our fair share. I remember my cousin getting clotheslined—literally by a clothesline—while riding a motorcycle at one of our Fourth of July picnics in Iowa. My mom grabbed a barbwire fence once while learning to ride a motorcycle and fiercely cut the inside of her hand. In one day, my uncle went through a barbwire fence on his dirt bike, my brother crashed while doing a wheelie on his dirt bike and fell over backward, and my sister crashed when the front tire fell off her minibike while jumping a ditch. That was a bad day at our house, but fortunately there were no major injuries to report.

Snapped back to reality with pain, I was worried sick about Matt and me. *Was Matt OK? Was I OK? What just happened? Should we call 911?* I could still hear people talking, but I couldn't comprehend what was being said. I just knew I had to figure this out so we could take the next step, whatever that was. My thoughts of calling 911 were bouncing back and forth in my head. If I called an ambulance, it would take them forever to get to us. We were remote, on Road 364 of North Divide Trail System in Teller County near Divide, Colorado. We were just west of Colorado Springs in the beautiful Rocky Mountains, directly north of Pikes Peak. Some people call it 717 Trails.

Whatever you call it, it was my favorite place to ride in the whole wide world. You get the both of best worlds—you can ride mellow and stay on the county dirt roads, challenge your skills through tough, bumpy, sketchy terrain trails, or certainly mix it up throughout your day by riding both. A little rough and tough was up my alley. I have always been a little of an adrenaline junkie, always up for a challenge. I would do a little scary riding at times then some easy stuff to get my heart rate back down and, of course, give my body a rest. Riding ATVs takes a lot of strength and endurance; it's hard on your entire body especially after a long day of riding. A typical ATV weighs about 500 pounds, so it takes some muscle to maneuver. Ever since I can remember, I liked adventure with physical activities, so ATVs were a good fit for me. Up until that point it had been a good purchase, and I rode a lot.

Think, Diane, think! Maybe we should get back on the ATV and ride out of here and back to the 357 Trailhead. Wait, the ATV. Where was the ATV? I looked across that brown, densely packed dirt road, and I saw my gray ATV upside down. My Suzuki King Quad 750 was on its top. I hoped she was OK. I don't like it when my stuff gets damaged. It was important to me to take care of the things I owned. My two ATVs were stored in the garage on their trailer and didn't sit outside in the weather when not being used. They got serviced and washed after every use; they were a little spoiled, I guess. Taking care of my stuff was a trait I learned from my family. As long as I can remember, my whole family took care of their toys. I remember my brother Danny teaching me, "Take care of your things and they will take care of you."

I looked over to my left where Matt and Chris were standing at the edge of that hard, dirt-packed road next to a little mud puddle, with a beautiful meadow and beaver ponds surrounded by pine trees in the background. Matt had mud all over his face that was running down his cheeks. He must have landed in that little-bitty mud puddle when we got bucked off the King Quad. Matt attempted to walk toward me, but he couldn't walk very well at all; he was hurt! *Oh shit. I hope he is OK.* I hate to see people hurt or in pain, especially someone I care for.

I am undeniably a helper, always have been and probably always will be. Maybe even a little on the enabler, co-dependent side. I like to help when loved ones are hurt. I want to fix it and make it all better. I want to be there to let them know I care and that I can help. I'm a *What can I do to make it better?* kind of person. I am not sure if I am so eager to help because I care for people more than myself or it's easier to worry about someone else's problems rather than my own. Looking back at my childhood, I craved to be important, to matter, to be nurtured, to be babied a little, so I go overboard to show people I care. Maybe if I did it for others, they will do it for me—treat others how you want to be treated.

I wished someone had been there for me a little more in my life, made me feel secure, loved, and important. As a child, I craved to feel special and matter to someone, anyone. Many times I felt like screaming at the top of my lungs, "Someone pay attention to me and love me." Logic would tell me those people should have been my parents, but I think I would have accepted it from anyone. When I started dating, I expected guys to make me feel important and special. I was starving for that kind of attention. I know my family cared, but only on a surface level. I wanted deep heartfelt love and attention. I was not aware of loving myself, so I constantly reached out for love and acceptance from others.

I turned my attention back to Matt. He was standing but not super straight. His left forearm had major road rash, and he still had wet, runny mud all over his face. His head seemed to be fine. I didn't see any cuts or bleeding from his head. His left leg was turned out sideways as he dragged it in an attempt to walk toward me. He stepped with his right and drug his left; he reminded me of the Hunchback of Notre Dame, all bent over and dragging his feet to walk. *Did he break his femur or his pelvis maybe? Holy crap my back hurts!* My breathing was getting harder to accomplish and much shallower. It took every ounce of energy to inhale. *When was the pain going to go away? When would my breathing return to normal?*

Instead of just thinking words, I finally spoke out loud. "We gotta get outta here and get help," I said, shocked by the words spoken in my own voice.

Once again, I had to think about what we were going to do. *I can use my cell phone to call an ambulance, but that will take forever. We are at least thirty minutes from the trailhead and another thirty minutes from the closest hospital. We can start heading back to the trailhead, call 911, and meet them on the trail or at the trailhead. No, wait. I've seen Flight for Life here before; maybe we can call them. I remember they had to come pick up a girl one time who fell off an ATV and broke her femur. No, neither one of us is hurt enough to bother those people from Flight for Life. Plus, they couldn't land at our location anyway, not enough room on this hard dirt road for a helicopter.* Somehow, I noticed it was a beautiful but chilly February day in Colorado with the brightest blue sky, no clouds, no wind. It was as calm as can be, very peaceful, both me and the weather.

We need to flip that ATV over and ride out, and we need to do it now. Matt and Chris continued to converse, although I had no idea what they were saying as I was in my own little world of thoughts about getting home. *I just want to go home. I am done there.*

"Can you and Chris flip this ATV back over?" I asked, taking charge of the situation and trying to solve our problem.

Problem solving and critical thinking are two of my strongest attributes. Some people refer to it as over thinking, but I like to be prepared. I like to know what is happening and what I am getting myself into before I get into it. Ironically, earlier in the day Matt and I were talking about getting into an ATV accident, and my big question was how do you prepare for that? Being unprepared has not ever been my forte. I like being prepared and knowing what is going on at all times. Is this a control issue? I am not sure. I just know I feel better and less stressed when I am prepared. Always knowing how to get out of a situation can be a very helpful skill. I don't feel I try to control the situation as much as be prepared if something goes wrong.

Matt and Chris flipped the King Quad back over, and I quickly checked it out to make sure it was in working, driving condition. The headlight cover was cracked, and the handle was ever so slightly bent, but it looked pretty healthy overall. I realized I had to get on that ATV and ride out. Fear never even entered my mind, but dread took over my thoughts because I knew getting on was not going to be easy, nor did we have a smooth ride back. Those dirt-packed roads were pretty bumpy. If I drove, I could hold on to the handlebars and not get bounced around too much. Bouncing around on the back of one of those things can be brutal when you're not hurt; there was no way I could endure that rough ride as a passenger. A comfortable ride home was all I wanted at this point.

Why is it when we're hurt or sick, we want to go home? Home definitely is a comfort zone for most. For me it was a safe place, for sure, but not in a comforting sort of way where I was going to get the nurturing I needed, just in a familiar place sort of way. It was like a hiding place where I could feel obscure. I didn't feel safe, secure, or confident about myself or anything else for that matter, especially when I was out in public, mainly in school. I never confessed to anyone how afraid I was of the outside. I just dealt with it, doing what I needed to do every day. My family didn't talk about things like feelings, thoughts, and, surely not, fears. We just had to be tough and not show many emotions. It was as if everything was going to be OK if we were tough.

"Do you mind if I drive?" I asked. "I think it'll be better if I can hold on. I think it will hurt less. Are you sure you're OK?"

"Yeah," Matt said, "I'm gonna be fine." He would never admit to not being fine. I am not sure if he really was fine or just saying that so I wouldn't worry. He's a very independent man, pretty much does his own thing and takes care of his own needs. He is not the type to say, "Hell no, I am hurt; take care of me." I needed to assume he was fine, although he didn't look that way as he proceeded to get on the ATV.

When Matt and I first met, I knew he was not a man of emotions—stoic and hard were more like him. I wasn't sure initially if that was going to be a good fit for me, as I had spent many painful years learning about my feelings and self-awareness through counseling, reading, meditation, and prayer. I knew where I stood, I was in touch with my thoughts and feelings, and I wanted someone in my life on that same page. He and I met on an online dating website, and I pretty much knew right away he was not a man who expressed his feelings, but there was something about him I liked. I never knew what he was thinking or how he felt about me, which left a lot to my imagination, especially with our relationship. I don't like reading into things because my imagination can get a little wild and negative sometimes. I like to know where I stand in situations, whether good or bad. Relationships are really pretty simple: If you want to be in one with me, act like it and show me love and respect. If you cannot show me love and respect, then move on. Matt may have known in his own mind what he was thinking and feeling toward me, but it didn't get expressed to me.

Although it was hard for me to tell what Matt's injuries were, I knew we needed to get moving. We needed to get on that Suzuki and start our way back to 357 Trailhead. We needed medical attention.

I could barely get on that beast. My entire body was not working right. I couldn't walk, I couldn't lift my left leg, and hell, I could hardly even breathe. But I was able to stand, and my brain was working fine; I was thankful to have found some positives in the moment. Thank God for helmets to protect my head and brain. I almost always rode with a helmet on and was very grateful I had mine on that day.

Being the determined, stubborn person I am, combined with knowing I had no other choice, I knew I must get on that ATV. I still wasn't scared or in panic mode; I remained calm as can be and knew what needed to be done. After what seemed like hours and in excruciating pain, I finally lifted my left leg high enough to step on the brake plate and swung my right leg over the seat to get on. *Whew, I made it.* I felt I had just accomplished a major feat.

I reached for the key and prayed that she started. Vroom ... she started right up. Those words from my brother rang in my head, "Take care of things, and they will take care of you." Suzuki makes an amazing ATV: durable, reliable, and indestructible. I was sad she had a cracked headlight cover and a few scratches, but super relieved she was in working order. For a split second, I had that thought of panic: *what would we have done if she didn't start?* Fortunately, we weren't faced with that obstacle. Starting the engine was more than half the battle. I knew we were going to make it to the truck.

"Can you lift your leg and climb on?" I asked Matt. He didn't look like he was doing very well; he looked like he had something broken for sure as he continued to struggle with his gait. I looked at the mud on his face along with a painful, maybe scared, scowl and wondered what happened to him in the crash. As he attempted to climb on, he grabbed my shoulders as I winced in pain; somehow, he managed to drag himself on behind me. I couldn't see exactly how he did it as I couldn't turn my body or twist to look behind me.

It seemed ironic Matt was relying on me to assist him on that ATV. Matt has muscles that have muscles. His body looks like that of the Incredible Hulk—not green just muscular. He towers over me by about eight inches and doubles my weight. We look like Beauty and the Beast together. Not that I consider myself beautiful, but I do consider him a beast!

So, off we went at a whopping 5 mph. Road 364 was where we crashed, a road I had traveled many times. However, it never seemed so rough or so long as it did that day. I swore we hit every bump, every dip, and every rock. I never had experienced such a rough, rattling ride—*maybe something was wrong with the ATV? Do my tires even have air?* It didn't seem like that kind of bumpy though. I've had my fair share of flat tires on those ATVs, so I was pretty familiar with flat-tire bumpy. I tried bending over to look down at them and was brought back to a painful reality that my body didn't move that way without enormous pain. I gave myself a little pep talk that it was going to be a rough ride and we had to keep trucking along. My mind kept saying over and over, *we can do this; we're going to be OK.*

As we crept along at about 10 mph, we kept asking one another if we were OK. We both kept saying, "Yeah,

I'm fine." Deep down I thought I was. I had no idea how badly hurt I actually was. Matt kept turning around to check on Chris who was on my other ATV behind us; it was also a King Quad but an army green 450. Suddenly Matt screamed at me, and I could not believe my ears.

"Stop," he yelled. "Chris just rolled!"

"No way!" I said with total, TOTAL disbelief. I simply refused to believe what I had just heard. I don't believe things very easily; typically I need to see to believe. I could tell by the seriousness in Matt's voice what he just said was true.

I have always had a difficult time with trust and faith, believing and understanding. I did not believe much and trusted nothing at all, not even myself. Although, as I have matured and studied both faith and trust, I have a better perception than when I was younger. I do believe they go hand in hand; you can't have one without the other, like the egg and the chicken ... which comes first, trust or faith? Even though you cannot physically see either one, I believe they are imperative to a stable foundation in many areas of life.

During my quest for understanding trust, I read an amazing book titled *Trust* by Iyanla Vanzant. I learned that not only do I need to have trust in others, but I need to trust myself. I was not even sure what trusting myself meant, but thought it was an interesting concept. I was aware that I needed to trust others, but never myself. I interpreted that book to mean I needed to trust myself and rely on myself just as I would trust and rely on others, believe in myself just as I would believe in others. I must trust my gut instincts to know right from wrong and good from bad. I definitely needed to trust my desires on how I want to be treated and trust knowing what I wanted in life. The book also talked about trusting in God, trusting in others, and trusting in life, which were not easy for me either. If you have not read this book, it is a must read, especially if you struggle with trust. I keep it close by and refer to it often.

I was in shock with the news I received from Matt about Chris. *There was no way, no possible flippin' way he had crashed! What the heck was going on here?* I had not crashed in all the years I owned the ATVs, and we were on our second one of the day. I stopped so Matt could climb off, which was no easy feat. It took all the energy and strength I had to stand up so he could get off. I realized again how much pain I was in and how I couldn't turn around. I tried with all my might to twist my body, to turn to see what was going on back there, trying to see if Chris was OK. My body did not allow for the twist, but it allowed me to rotate my head just enough to see out of the corner of my eye, to see my other King Quad on its side.

Chris stood there shaking his head, and Matt drug his left leg like the Hunchback to go to his aid. I felt so bad for Matt; he was obviously hurt. I also had concern that Chris was OK from his crash and wondered what happened. We needed to get Matt to an ER; he obviously had something broken as he couldn't walk very well. The thought of getting to an ER wasn't about me; it was about getting Matt the help he needed. After all, I thought I was fine. I just knocked the wind out of myself and maybe a had a broken rib or two.

No way, I kept thinking. *No Way, No Way, No Way!* I turned back around and just waited. I was helpless, no tears, no panic. If I used my strength and energy to get off that beast, I was afraid I would not be able to get back on. Helpless. I just sat there and waited. *Hurry though,* I quietly thought. I could not breathe well, and it hurt.

"Quit fucking around; we need to get her to the hospital!" Matt screamed to Chris. Matt has a very deep, loud voice that carries, so I was pretty sure everyone in the town of Divide heard him as well.

I was tickled Matt screamed at Chris; he was concerned for me, and that was so sweet. *He really did care for me!* Matt didn't show his loving emotions for me on a regular basis, so I was impressed; it made me feel important to him, like I did matter. As I said Matt is the type who believes it's not appropriate to show emotion, especially sappy, love type of feelings — at least that was my experience thus far into our relationship. Did he not show it because he really didn't feel it, or did he just suck at showing mushy stuff? That had been an ongoing question so far into my relationship with Matt, and it drove me absolutely crazy. I tried hard not to read too much into it, but I also liked to know where I stood. *Just tell me; show me if you love me. It is not that hard.* He seemed to express his disappointment or anger, so I knew those emotions were present but not mushy stuff. I hoped he cared and just sucked at showing it. I have discovered throughout our relationship he showed he cared through hard work. Being a hard worker is extremely important to him.

Oh no, he's back. That meant I had to stand up again so he could get back on. Was this pain ever going to stop? It seemed to be getting worse not better. And I was soooo thirsty, it was painful. I didn't even have enough spit to swallow. My tongue was stuck to the roof of my mouth and felt like the Mohave Desert in there. I wondered what happened to all my saliva; it was beyond a weird experience. Evidently, I was experiencing several new things that February day. As a dental hygienist, I have encountered many patients over the years who suffered from dry mouth and that obviously must be what they felt like. Poor things. I must have more sympathy for them in the future—what a horrible feeling. I literally could not swallow. I had nothing for moisture. I felt like I just licked a dirt road.

"Is he OK?" I asked.

"Yeah, he's fine. I told him to quit fucking around; we need to get you to the hospital," he said.

I didn't know Chris very well at all; he was a friend of Matt's I had met only once before. In fact, the one and only time I was in a boat accident, Chris was also with us. As far as I am concerned, Chris is a bad omen and not allowed to go with us anymore. Evidently Chris was screwing around on the way back to the car, went slowly up an embankment, and rolled the ATV. Not very cool to do when two people are hurt and in major need of medical treatment. In fact, not very cool to do at all. *Why would he treat my stuff like that?* Just because I would never treat someone's stuff like that, I thought Chris should have that same concept. How disrespectful of him to drive carelessly. I was grateful he wasn't hurt but upset he disrespected my ATV. I expected him to know better.

I believe expectations will get us in trouble every time. I learned several years ago one reason we get mad, upset, frustrated, or sad is because of our expectations. When we assume that certain things are going to happen and it doesn't go as we "expect," we get upset. We get mad when someone doesn't do or act in the way we think they should or that we "expect" them to. I cannot even begin to tell you how many times I was disappointed because of this little concept. I go through every day, every week, and every month with expectations; some get met and some do not. I continue to focus on not expecting people to do what I would do.

Thankfully, Matt climbed back on the ATV without causing too much pain for either one of us. The last thing we needed was more pain and more struggle, although things were going pretty smoothly considering everything that had happened so far. I am truly grateful things were not worse.

"Maybe you should ride side saddle," I told him. I was glad to see I still had my sense of humor. I had to laugh to myself, and I was pretty sure a smile came across my face. I've been known to have a great sense of humor. Ever since I can remember, laughing and joking around have been a big part of who I am. I know when and where to be serious and when to be funny. I reminded myself it was time for serious again as we putted along.

My mouth was still like a desert. I badly needed water. We always rode with food and water just in case we got stranded. I did not want to stop again, so I asked Matt to hand me our water that was in the drink holder. It did not even come close to quenching my thirst. My mouth was drier than that dirt road we were on.

That ride back to the trailhead never seemed so far; surely, we had been riding for hours by now. Some parts of the trail were icy, snowy, and muddy so we couldn't go very fast. But I knew with our physical condition we couldn't go very fast anyway.

About twenty minutes into the ride, we finally came to the main road, Teller County Road 357. It was a typical county dirt road in the Rocky Mountains, wide enough for two cars, a little rutted and a little bumpy with lots of little rocks and hard, packed dirt, and very well maintained. It was a winding, twisty, hilly gravel road surrounded by pine trees. It was mostly dry for February; usually there are patches of snow. Seeing Road 357 meant the trailhead was just a few minutes away. *Thank God, we're going to make it!*

However, the thought of not making it hadn't crossed my conscious mind, but somehow my subconscious mind was a little more relieved to confirm the trailhead really WAS just around the corner. Some people might have given up hope out there on the trail, freaked out, panicked, and even lost their minds, but I never lost hope; I knew we would make it. That could have been naïve thinking or unrealistic thinking on my part, but deep down inside I knew it was going to be OK. Maybe it was the power of my positive thinking. For the most part I am pretty positive in situations. I believe it will all be good and believe in the best until proved otherwise. Plus, I don't give up easily, I am relentless most of the time, I fight until the bitter end, and I don't take no or can't for an answer.

We pulled into the parking lot at the trailhead. I got off the ATV and suggested to the guys they ask Dave for help loading the machines. Dave was a gentleman we met when we arrived at the trailhead who owns an ATV store in town. Although I had confidence in Matt and Chris to load the ATVs; they were a bit unfamiliar with the process.

I had a double trailer where one ATV loaded from the side and one from the rear. They pretty much will only fit one way, so I knew they could figure it out—plus, they're guys.

"I'm going to the truck," I said.

My walking ability was unquestionably impaired. Even though my legs felt fine, my back did not. Lifting my left leg up to take a step was almost impossible for me. My back was badly hurt; the pain was killing me— perhaps literally, I was not sure. It was hard to breathe, and I thought I was going to throw up it hurt so much. I have never experienced that amount of pain. It was like the motor function was gone on the left side of my body, plus I barely had the strength or energy to drag my leg. I too looked like the Hunchback. My posture was definitely compromised, I drug my leg as I walked, and I could barely breathe. I didn't think I was going to make it 20 feet to the cab of the truck. I felt the crowd of people just standing there staring at me. Not one person asked if they could help. I guess I expected someone to at least offer some assistance; it was obvious something bad had happened. I was not even sure what anyone could have done, but at least they could ask. Again, I was "expecting" people to do what I would have done.

Oh man! I suddenly realized I had to get myself into that lifted Dodge truck. Those running boards seemed high under normal conditions, but that day they were extremely high. They seemed up over my head, like the beanstalk Jack had to climb. I reached my hands up to take off my helmet and realized for the first time my left arm didn't want to cooperate very well at all. I could barely move it because the pain was so incredible. It was like a knife was stabbing me in the back and an elephant was sitting on my chest. My right arm worked great, so I single-handedly wiggled my helmet back and forth to get it off, scraping my ears only a little. Ripping off my ears was the least of my worries at that point. Those helmets fit fairly tight, but I was grateful I had mine on.

My mind kicked back in and pushed on to *We have to, we must get in that truck.* The pain in my whole body was so strong, especially in my back. For the first time there were a few split-second thoughts that I was not going to make it. I thought I might die! I started to feel something major was wrong; my breathing was more painful and severely shallow. People don't live through this much pain, do they? I knew I was not ready to die. I still had too many things to accomplish. I have two boys I needed to stick around for, I needed to see my youngest graduate high school, I needed to see my boys get married, and I needed to be a grandmother. *Hang in there, kiddo, you're going to be OK.*

I have been bucked off a horse, have straddled a balance beam, labored through two childbirths, but none of those painful experiences even came close to what I was going through. I tried not to focus on what was the most pain I had ever been in and tried to focus on what needed to be done.

I made it. I got in the truck! I watched Matt struggle getting in. His left leg was not functioning very well, and I could tell by the scowl on his face that he was deep with pain and concern.

"Are you OK?" I asked.

"Fuck no. I'm hurt!" he replied in a very deep, matter-of-fact manner. He seemed angry, pissed off, and frustrated. I wasn't sure if he was angry at me or the situation, and, of course, I felt bad. I hated to see people in pain. He was annoyed, but he gets annoyed easily. He often speaks in that tone of voice, so it wasn't out of the ordinary. However, I knew he was in pain by his facial expressions. I knew not to say anything more. I just sat there and watched him struggle getting in. I wanted to help him but certainly was not in any position to be of any assistance. It was hard to watch.

I was confused, I knew what was going on but at the same time felt I was stumbling through a slow-motion movie where everything was dragging along. You know the man's deep voice that talks tremendously slowly? Reminds me of playing a record on the wrong speed and all the words are long and drawn out. I felt like I was trying to focus on what was really happening at the moment, but I also had no idea what that was. I felt connected and disconnected at the same time. I guess it was safe to say I was in a state of confusion. The mind is an amazing thing.

As we pulled away from the trailhead, it dawned on me I had new insurance I hadn't used before. I wondered if I could go to any facility. I reached for my insurance card and phone to find out. I needed to know what ER to go to. Matt could go anywhere with his insurance, but I had Kaiser and thought I had to go to one of their facilities.

We discussed going to the nearest ER, which was in Woodland Park, or driving all the way to Denver because of my insurance. I tried several times to contact someone within the Kaiser network but kept getting the recording for the automated service. It was a Saturday, and I really didn't expect anyone to answer. We finally decided to go to the nearest emergency room in Woodland Park, which was only about thirty minutes away. Looking back, this was a major blessing in disguise as I had no idea of the extent of my injuries.

I considered calling my boys and my family to tell them what happened but decided to wait to see what was going on first. I was pretty sure I had just broken a couple of ribs and knocked the wind out of myself. *I'll just call them on the way home. This ER trip shouldn't be long.*

The ER

*"Trust the Lord with all your heart and don't depend
on your own understanding"*

—PROVERBS 3:5-6

MY BIOLOGICAL FATHER WAS AN ALCOHOLIC and my
mom kicked him out of the house after eighteen years
of marriage. I was only one year old, so I didn't even
remember him. I never referred to "Adam" as my dad,
he was just a sperm donor to me, nothing more. I did
not know him, and I had no contact with him. When my
mom divorced him, he pretty much went away and left
us alone. One of my sisters used to tell me stories about
Adam being the town drunk and how uncomfortable
it was for them in school because everybody knew it. I
have always felt sad for my siblings who had to endure

a drunk for a dad and the embarrassment they must have faced. Of course, I was so grateful I didn't have to deal with that. I could not imagine how awkward and degrading that must have been.

My mom was thirty-five years old and a single mom with seven kids when she divorced Adam. I cannot imagine what she must have been going through at that time, but I've always had so much respect for her. She worked three jobs to support us and kept all seven kids together. We were so fortunate and grateful that we didn't get pawned off on the state as many kids do. My mother has always put her kids first and did more for her kids than she did for herself. I admire my mother to this day for the love of her children and for providing us with all our basic needs; however, I secretly wished she would have been more nurturing and loving to fill my insecurities.

It was 1968 when she met this man named Dave. Dave was twelve years younger than my mom, but they started dating and married anyway. At twenty-three, Dave was only five years older than my oldest brother, Joe. Need I remind you this was in a predominantly Catholic community in Iowa? Divorce was majorly frowned upon, much less marrying a non-Catholic that was twelve years younger. I cannot imagine what my mother experienced, so again I have a lot of respect for her bravery. She was not welcomed in the church any longer but continued living her life and taking care of us.

I always thought the youngest two of us kids were so lucky not having to tolerate our father much. We weren't affected by his absence much, or so I thought. Little did I know EVERYONE is affected by an alcoholic parent even at a very young age. I have had my fair share of issues; however, I do not blame all of my shortcomings on an alcoholic father, but I do know some issues stem from abandonment by a parent.

When we pulled into the hospital Emergency parking lot, Matt drove right up to the doors—truck, trailer, and all. He threw the truck in park and came around to help me get out. Oh my gosh, I was in so much pain. *What was going on here? It was getting worse not better. Why couldn't I walk? Why was I hurting? Why couldn't I breathe?* There was the thought again that I was going to die. Something had to be seriously wrong, and I knew it. I now knew it was a little more than a broken rib. Breathing was so painful that I couldn't stand it anymore. The pain to walk was more than excruciating. I thought I was going to crumble. I was starting to think the worst. *Snap out of it; stop being a sissy. Suck it up, sister, and get your ass into that ER.* There I went again with the self-talk.

Growing up as a sissy was not an option in my house. I was very much a tomboy and not much of a girly-girl at all. I wore a dress only when I absolutely had to; otherwise you could pretty much find me in jeans and a T-shirt. Being tough was the preference in my family, for both the boys and girls. I am not sure if this was pounded in my head or just an observed learned behavior. I do know we were not babied when hurt. I was raised very old school; you didn't cry or admit you were hurt; you threw some dirt on it, shook it off, and kept on going. My whole family was pretty active and adventurous—and tough, of course. We played with firecrackers, tried out our dad's cigarettes in the hayloft, and rode bicycles on frozen ponds. We definitely put ourselves at risk for injuries.

We finally made it inside the ER where I heard people asking what happened.

"We were in an ATV accident!" Matt said.

"How fast were you going?" someone asked.

"About 20, maybe 25, I don't know for sure," Matt said.

They sat me down in one of the chairs at the first check-in desk. The gentleman asked for an insurance card and driver's license as a lady went to get a wheelchair. Matt left to go move the truck, and that was the last I saw of him for what seemed like days.

"I can't breathe," I told them firmly, almost panicked. "I'm in a lot of pain and I need help." The man was still asking for my identification and insurance information. I handed him my entire wallet. "Here, take what you need, I don't care," I said.

"I'm in pain, a lot of pain, and I need help!" I demanded. "I CANNOT BREATHE!" I screamed as best I could. I was running out of air.

The woman came back with a wheelchair and decided to take me back to the treatment room before check-in was complete. She asked again how fast we were going.

I told her, "I have no idea, maybe 20, 25 mph. We weren't going all that fast. We went over a small jump and rolled or something."

She helped me stand from the wheelchair and started taking my clothes off. Anyone who knows me, knows I dress in layers when it is cold. Heck, even when it is not cold, I am in layers. I had on a coat, a heavy sweater, and my Ibex thermals (I love my Ibex). She had a heck of a time getting those garments off because my left side was pretty much paralyzed at that point. Excruciating pain took over in my back as we struggled, and I continued wincing in pain. The nurse was awesome as she managed to get the items over my head without having to cut them off. I've seen on television where they have to cut your clothes off sometimes to expose your body; I'm glad she didn't have to do that. She told me she didn't like to ruin people's clothes, so she was going to do her best to not cut them. She also had no idea of the extent of my injuries; otherwise I'm pretty sure she wouldn't have risked hurting me further and would have cut off all my clothes.

After what seemed like hours getting off my tops, she moved on to my riding boots and jeans. This wasn't going to be easy, but again she did a wonderful job. I tried to help as much as I could, but I wasn't very success-ful. I had on riding boots considered to be high-tops that needed to be totally unlaced to get them off, even on a good day. I had on Ibex thermals under my jeans, too. Those peeled off like a green onion as they rolled back on themselves while she went along undressing me.

She helped me get onto the bed as she continued to ask questions: What happened? How fast were you going? Were you driving? Was he drinking? How fast were you going? Where does it hurt? Do you know where you are? How fast were you going? I was very coherent and able to answer all the questions. For some reason, they were very interested in how fast we were going. *For fuck sake, ask me a different question,* I thought to myself, *I do not know exactly how fast we were going.*

I spoke outload and continued to explain that I had not been driving, and I had no idea how fast we were going. Matt was driving, he was not drinking or even driving stupid; we went over a small jump and crashed — that's all I knew. I didn't know how we landed, if the ATV landed on me, or if we even rolled. I had absolutely no idea of the details. It all happened so fast! I just knew I was badly hurting, I was in agony, and I could not breathe! My words were slow and meticulous this time to make sure she understood what I knew and to stop asking me how fast we were going.

I felt the ER staff hooking up blood pressure cuffs and taking my temperature as they continued to make small talk: Do you live in Woodland Park? Where are you from? What do you do for work? When did you eat last? What did you have to eat? Are you allergic to anything?

They started an IV as they explained, "We are going to have to do some CAT scans with this contrast dye, so we can get a really good picture of what is going on inside."

I told them I was extremely thirsty and asked if I could have a drink of water. As the words came out of my mouth, I already knew the answer was going to be NO! I knew at that point they might have to sedate me. I was not getting any water; they just asked me when the last time I ate was. I knew that meant sedation and no water or food.

"No water," they said. "Not until we know what's going on."

We rolled down the hall in my ER bed to the imaging department. I was by myself because Matt was getting looked at as well. Chris kept bouncing back and forth between my room and his, but I had no idea where he was at that moment. I wasn't stressed or nervous, but I was a little scared for the first time—just a little and it only lasted a second. I was in survival mode, just doing what they told me I needed to do. I lay there with no emotions whatsoever.

I got to the machine for CT scans and realized I could not even lift my head, much less pick myself up to scoot over onto the bed. I lay there totally motionless. Oh my gosh, I hoped I wasn't paralyzed. I hoped this lack of movement was only temporary. I expressed my concern to the technician that I couldn't move to get on that bed, and I felt my heartbeat start to accelerate.

The tech asked, "You must be, what, a buck 15? Could I just pull the sheet and slide you on over? There's going to be a bit of a bump," he said.

A bump? That was a bit of an understatement. It felt like he just pulled me over Mount Everest. My back felt it all, every inch.

He asked what happened. "We were in an ATV accident," I replied.

"Oh my gosh, I had an ATV roll over on me once while hunting, flipped right over on top of me," he said. "Those things are so fun but so dangerous. Did it land on you?"

I was just waiting for him to ask me how fast I was going. Fortunately, he did not, because I wasn't sure I could take it one more time. I was not sure if that made me feel better or worse to hear his story. Obviously, he lived to tell about it, so that was pretty cool. I would tend to think if an ATV flipped over on you, it would crush you and kill you.

"Oh yeah, we were lucky that it didn't land on us," I said, making an assumption. I still had no idea the extent of my injuries or even what happened for sure.

Thankfully, I have not had much experience with hospitals: two childbirths and a few trips to the ER for minor injuries. I have never had a horrible experience that made me hate hospitals. I always thought they were good places and were there to help people. Actually, I was intrigued by hospitals and why all the patients were actually there. Medicine and health have been passions of mine. I love learning about medical terminology, procedures, and protocol.

I lay there on my back as still as ever. I closed my eyes as they put the contrast into my IV. The tech explained to me it was going to feel like a really warm sensation throughout my entire body and that I might wet my pants. Boy, he wasn't kidding; that warm feeling was unusual and weird, something I had never experienced. I was a virgin to CAT scans and contrast dye. Generally, I am a little claustrophobic, but I was doing great. I was calm as he slid my bed into the tunnel like a conveyer belt. Although my mind raced a bazillion thoughts at once, I remained peaceful and closed my eyes. I might have been in shock; I was not sure.

"OK," he said, "we are done. I'm going to slide you back over those bumps and get you back on your bed."

Those words "your bed" kind of lingered in my head. I obviously had been there long enough for the bed to be called "mine." As he slid me back over those bumps, my entire backside was badly hurt. And I still could not breathe. I obviously had knocked the wind out of myself, but I wondered why breathing was still so difficult. I wondered why it was not back to normal yet and wondered why nobody was addressing the fact I COULD NOT BREATHE! I never really tried to self-diagnose my condition, which was very rare for me; usually I try to figure out what was wrong before the doctors tell me. It's kind of a challenge for me to see if I'm right or not. I was lost for a diagnosis this time but was now certain it had to be more than broken ribs and interrupted breathing.

I was back in my ER room for only a second when Chris came in. There was still no word on Matt or his injuries, but they had him in for x-rays.

As I lay there flat on my back, I could not tell if my eyes were open, but I really couldn't see much of anything, maybe some fluorescent lights? I was fading fast. I was not sure at that point what was going on. *Was I dreaming? Was I sedated? What next?* All I could do was wonder, all alone.

I was startled when the action around me kicked into high gear. A nurse was taking off my jewelry in a hurried manner like she was trying to win a race where the best time won. A very sweet nurse was calmly and carefully cutting off my sports bra, trying so hard to not ruin it while hurrying as well. I think she was racing the nurse taking off my jewelry, but she didn't want to show her competitive nature. I had told her it was my CU (University of Colorado) sports bra and one of my favorites so she would take extra caution removing it. Another nurse was explaining to me she needed to start a catheter while ripping packages open ferociously. *Wow, was she in the race, too?* Someone else was hooking up those sticky electrodes to my chest with one hand and a blood pressure cuff and a pulse oximeter with the other. These people were not messing around. I lay there motionless and patiently waited for instructions on what to do. I never went into panic mode, which was a huge surprise to me. There was a lot going on and I wondered if I should be in distress. *Was I dying? Was I going to be OK?* I was very proud of myself and kind of shocked that I remained calm. With all that was happening, I think anyone would panic; after all, hospitals can be dreadful.

I was brought back to reality abruptly when I heard a man's voice say, "Hi, I am Dr. Richardson. I'm a trauma surgeon here. It looks like you have a couple of broken ribs and you ruptured your spleen. We're going to have to do a little surgery to repair your spleen. I don't think we can do it laparoscopically, so I'll have to make a little incision on your belly." He held up his fingers to indicate a two- to three-inch incision. "Then we're going to transport you; you will need to be monitored for a few days."

He then asked, "Where do you live?"

"Southeast Denver area, Centennial," I replied.

He proceeded to tell me Colorado Springs had a great post-trauma department, and I would be in good hands there. He added they get a significant amount of dirt bike and ATV victims.

"Then let's go to the Springs," I told him. I honestly had no idea what was in store for me. I just had learned that I was an ATV victim with a few broken ribs and a ruptured spleen. Although it still wasn't clear to me what was going on and exactly what happened, I knew I wanted the best looking out for me. *Why is my surgeon wearing jeans and a T-shirt? And where are his scrubs?* Of all the things going on in my head, I wondered about my surgeon's attire? Some people might find that strange; however, I follow the rules pretty well and knew he was not dressed appropriately for a hospital, let alone surgery. *Was he real? Was this a dream?* I wasn't sure what was going on, but I did know I was about to have some sort of surgery.

I believe my Catholic upbringing taught me structure and discipline in many areas. Following the rules and protocol was a big deal to me. Tell me what the rules are, and I am all in. I don't like or appreciate when details are left out. I am not a big fan of making the rules, but I am a huge advocate of following them. Abiding by a dress code certainly fits into my idea of rules. In parochial school we, of course, had to wear uniforms every day; ours was a blue plaid jumper with a white dress shirt. I never once challenged the dress code or tried to cheat on that. Secretly, I was deathly afraid of going to hell if I rocked the boat; it was just easier to do what I was told.

As a professional in the dental field, I have had my fair share of dress requirements, wearing scrubs almost every day of my working career. I often wondered if I chose my career subconsciously based on there being a strict dress code.

To this day, clothes are not important to me. I see them as a necessity, not a luxury. I like workout clothes the best. I don't particularly like dressing up, never have. Scrubs, workout gear, or jeans make up most of my wardrobe. I'm not sure why I have a whole closet full of dress clothes—other than I might need them someday.

The ICU

"I opened two gifts this morning.
They were my eyes."

—ANONYMOUS

QUESTIONING THE SURGEON'S ATTIRE was the last thing I remember until I woke up, thrashing like a fish out of water trying to get that awful tube out of my mouth and throat. I was not sure what it was, but I knew I did not like it. I asked Matt to get the nurse—I wanted that out! I tried pulling it out myself. Saying I was disoriented would have been an understatement. I did not have a clue where I was and what was going on, but, trust me, I wanted to know everything. I'm a detail-oriented person: Tell me everything, good and bad; I need to know it all. Even though things were very blurry,

I could tell I was in a hospital, maybe in an operating room. I could see a lot of big, bright lights above me and hear beeping noises everywhere. I couldn't move and felt like I was suffocating, as I couldn't breathe through my mouth or nose. I was positive there were heavy weights on my chest. *What was up with this breathing issue?* Something had changed in my breathing, my chest and back no longer hurt, but I was being smothered.

Matt and a nurse were standing there staring down at me; based on their expressions, I wasn't sure who was more confused, me or them. *Oh, good Lord, where was I and what was wrong?* I tried asking where I was, what had happened, but it was only a thought in my head. I could not turn those thoughts into words; I could not speak. Thoughts just sat there swirling around in my head. A sense of panic stirred in me with a strong sense of the need to know what the hell was going on. I had something big, bulky, and totally awkward in my mouth making it next to impossible to breathe and certainly impossible to talk.

The nurse and Matt had no idea what I was trying to ask, as I continued mouthing words over and over. I was starting to get frustrated; all I wanted to know was where I was … why was this so difficult? I lay there trying to figure out how to communicate with these people, but obviously what I was doing was to no avail. I held up my first three fingers. I could see Matt and the nurse. "See" was something of an exaggeration; they were a little out of focus as my eyes darted back and forth from one to the other trying to establish something stable. I had no idea what they were thinking. I couldn't make out a facial expression well enough to get any information. They just stared at me speechless waiting for me to make my next move.

"Three!" Matt and the nurse exclaimed. They were so proud of themselves, like they just got the right answer on *Jeopardy*.

I shook my head back and forth as best I could with all those restraints to indicate "no" and again held up the same first three fingers of my right hand.

"Three?" they asked, this time sounding a little defeated.

I shook my head again, back and forth, trying harder this time to make it go side to side. My frustration level was on the rise, and I am sure I had a deep scowl on my face. *This is a "W" people, not a "3." Sheesh!!*

Spell out the whole word, my brain said. So I held up the three fingers again, then continued to hold out two fingers sideways, then folded my fingers in. I tried to spell out "where."

"Sign language, she's doing sign language!" they exclaimed. They were all excited again; they figured it out; they got the question correct.

Finally, they understood what I was doing. There was a little relief on both sides, probably more on mine than theirs. I shook my head in an up and down motion indicating "yes" as best I could. From what I could tell, there was a little relief in their eyes as if I was communicating with them. My head was strictly restrained for some strange reason and movement was limited at best.

I heard them talking to each other. "I don't know sign language; do you know sign language?" Neither one knew it, so they were not sure what I was trying to say or spell out. They were conversing back and forth over me as if I wasn't even there. If I could have slapped my hand to my forehead, I would have. I finally got them to see I was doing sign language, but they didn't know it. Disappointment and frustration set in. *Now what? Now how am I going to communicate?* I could not see them any longer because I closed my eyes to regain my thoughts. *Back to the drawing board.* I felt defeated, and I don't like to lose. It seemed like hours had gone by, and I still had no idea where I was and what was going on, but I was suffocating.

Competitiveness is a strong trait used to describe me. In pretty much every aspect of my life, I compete. Mostly within myself. Always trying to do better, go faster, be smarter. As long as I can remember, this has been a big part of my life. In school I always tried to get a higher score, a better grade, or more A's on my report card. Good was never good enough for me. I wanted to be the best I could be. I wasn't looking for perfect, just best. No matter what I seemed to do, I was not happy with good. I NEEDED best.

In sports, I wasn't ever where I wanted I to be. I wanted better than what I was. I wanted to be the best I could be. Looking back at various parts of my life, I knew with all my heart I didn't put forth 110%, and that is a regret I have lived with all my life, especially with gymnastics. I could have given more. I could have given 120%. I should have strived for more difficult routines, but I was afraid of getting hurt, I guess. I don't like pain, physical or mental, so I held back not giving it my all. I wished I could go back and do it over. I would try harder. I would do better.

The nurse eventually handed me a pen and paper, telling me to write down what I was trying to spell. I tried to write, "Where am I?"

She couldn't read my writing! Of course, she couldn't; can you imagine what that scribble must have looked like? I was extremely loopy from drugs, and I had more things hooked up to my face than I could ever have dreamed of; plus, my head and one arm were strapped down. No wonder she couldn't read my writing. I couldn't see, and I was shaky and dopey.

I felt disappointed and super frustrated as I realized I was not going to get the answers I needed. I could not scream, punch the pillow or run. I had absolutely no choice but to lie there. I lost the fight to communicate. I was defeated. I closed my eyes, isolated and abandoned.

I woke up startled and panicked because I couldn't breathe. Once again, I couldn't breathe! That was becoming quite the norm for me, struggling to breathe. I wondered at what point I was just going to stop with the battle altogether. *What was trying to kill me? I was being suffocated!* I tried pulling that awful beast-like tube out of my mouth again. I was going to die if I did not remove it. Suddenly people rushed to my bedside and tied down my arms and restrained me. I couldn't even thrash my head back and forth, as it was stabilized, too. *Oh shit. I was not going to like this. I couldn't be tied down. I couldn't be restrained. I could not breathe.* I wanted to panic. I was going to die. *Somebody please help me.* All I heard was talk about medicating me to keep me quiet through the night. *What the hell was going on? What on earth had happened? Was I still on Earth or did I die?*

I woke up in a hospital, where things were extremely fuzzy for what seemed like hours, maybe even days. I was so out of it. I had lost track of what day it was, what time it was, and I still had no idea where I was. I saw my two boys, Matthew and Hunter, alongside Matt. My arms were still strapped to my sides, I had that awful tube in my mouth and down my throat. I felt tremendously claustrophobic. I tried hard to talk to my boys, but the words didn't seem to come out right, if at all. I had no idea if I was even talking or just making sounds.

I could tell by the concerned look on their faces that my situation was not good. *My condition must be bad.* They both had frowns, looking as if they were very confused and hurt. I could see the hurt in their eyes! There were no tears as far as I could tell, but there was huge sadness and worry. *Oh, my goodness, what was wrong with me? What have I done?* They stared at me with a blank look, not knowing what to do or say, kind of like the deer-in-the-headlight look. I knew they would both do anything to make me all better if they could. I tried to communicate to them through my eyes. I tried to read the distressed look on their faces and reassure them I was going to be OK. Maybe I was looking at them to reassure me I was going to be OK; I wasn't even sure. There were times I thought I might die and that scared me. I was scared for them; I did not want them to lose their mom, as they were only eighteen and twenty-three at the time.

Matt had texted my boys from Woodland Park ER to tell them we were in an ATV accident and we thought I had broken a couple of ribs. Forty-five minutes later he told them to get to a Colorado Springs hospital, where I was being airlifted. I cannot even fathom what my boys were going through, and it breaks my heart to try to imagine. To this day, the pain and hurt my boys experienced still makes me cry; they hurt to see me hurt. I have thought about their pain almost every single day since the debacle on February 14, 2015. When they saw me as I got out of the Flight for Life helicopter, they probably thought I was going to die. I have had several conversations with both boys since that day and know what happened scared them. Whenever I see a Flight for Life helicopter, I have very conflicting emotions and

I cry. I am happy and grateful for such equipment and medical staff, knowing they are saving someone because that someone was me one time. Knowing they save lives makes me ecstatic. And, of course, I am so sad for those who don't make it. Everyone knows what it means when Flight for Life is called; it can go one of two ways. It is the true definition of bittersweet for me.

I don't know what Matt was thinking or feeling; as I've said he's not much for words or showing emotion. He, too, just stared at me without saying much. I never saw a tear, just major concern on his face. *Was he hurt? Was he scared?* I couldn't tell, and he gave me no signs of his feelings. I am sure he felt bad for what happened because he was driving; however, I was not blaming him, and I never will. It was not his fault at all; it was an accident, and I never wanted him to feel guilty. I just wanted him to love me, hug me gently, and reassure me everything was going to be OK. I wanted him to make me feel better. I wanted him to love me. I'm not saying he didn't love me, but I wanted to see it, to feel it. I was so fragile and weak mentally, emotionally, and certainly physically.

I used to work for an orthodontist who taught me, "There are no accidents!" Although I do think everything happens for a reason, those words kept ringing in my ears. So, what did that mean? Was there a reason for my injuries? Was there a reason we crashed? That concept was too much for me mentally to comprehend. I needed to focus on my physical healing to get out of that hospital. I wanted to go home, but I was scared I couldn't take care of myself yet. *Who was going to take care of me?* I still had no clue what was wrong with me, and I hadn't even walked yet. *Shit, can I even walk? Am I paralyzed?*

Finally, that nasty, bulky obnoxious tube that had been suffocating me for days was removed. I was so glad to get that out, but if there's a next time, I want to remain sedated when they remove it. Feeling that thing coming up out of my throat was horrible. It made me cough, gag, and almost puke. It felt as large and long as a garden hose. Did I mention it was AWFUL? They also unstrapped my arms. I was free and felt like I had accomplished something great. *I should be out of here in no time.*

In spite of being loopy, I decided to text my family and tell them I had been in an ATV accident. I still wasn't sure of all the details but knew I had to let my family know. The text conversations with my siblings were a little confusing. I couldn't seem to focus on anything yet and still did not have the whole story of what happened. All I knew was I had been in an ATV accident, had my spleen removed, and had "a few" broken ribs, but still had no clue on the full extent of my injuries. Heck, I was not even sure how many days had gone by.

One of my sisters, Lynn, called me right away and wanted ALL the details. She wanted to know everything, and I knew nothing. She asked a series of questions so fast I couldn't have answered under normal conditions.

What happened? Where are you? Who were you with? Where are the boys? Are you OK? Are they OK? Where are you? She obviously had no idea I wasn't able to think that clearly or that fast, but the questions kept coming.

Lynn is the second oldest daughter. She has a heart of gold and is very caring and super protective of me. Although she is eleven years older than I am, she and I are very close; she's probably the closest person to me in my life. Growing up, Lynn and I didn't have much of a connection at all; I'm sure some of it was the age gap. I cannot recall if it was a specific incident or just over time through talking that we developed the relationship we have now. I don't feel like we have a lot in common, but that has not stopped us from being close emotionally. She is a strong Christian woman and has helped me more than once learn about God, love, and forgiveness. Obviously, I'm still a work in progress—especially with the forgiveness part. I love her dearly and appreciate her more than she will ever know. I do tell her frequently how I feel about her.

Through my self-help journey I discovered I am very bad at forgiving people, especially myself. I knew you were supposed to forgive others but did not realize until later in life you should forgive yourself as well. My whole family is bad at forgiveness, others and themselves. I think it was a learned behavior not to or maybe I should say it was a behavior I never learned. We weren't taught how to forgive nor the importance of it. Although it is not easy for me to forgive people, it is easy for me to hold a grudge forever.

I didn't know where I was exactly. I knew in a hospital in Colorado Springs. I didn't know the name of the hospital or even what room number I was in. As I continued to talk with Lynn, I told her I ruptured my spleen, but it was no big deal; I'd be out in a few days. She again asked where I was, and she was baffled that I didn't know.

"How do you not know? Are you lying to me?" she asked.

"No!" I replied. "I really, truly have no clue what hospital I am in. I just know I am in Colorado Springs."

"What the heck are you doing in Colorado Springs? Where were you? Were the boys with you? What happened? Are you OK?" She rattled off those questions all over again, and I still could not think that fast. I am surprised she didn't ask how fast I was going! That seemed to be a pretty important question. I told her that was where they airlifted me, and I thought she was going to climb right through the phone.

I was all alone in my room so I promised her I would find out more details and call her back as soon as I could.

What seemed like days went by before I talked to the surgeon who was overseeing me during my stay in the hospital. Turns out, it had only been two days. Fortunately, he had answers for me and this was what I discovered: I was airlifted from UC Health Pikes Peak

Regional Hospital in Woodland Park to UC Health Memorial Hospital in Colorado Springs. I had eight broken ribs on the back, left side of my body; two fractured vertebrae; a ruptured spleen; and a puncture in my left lung. Oh yeah, and I had had a blood transfusion, was in ICU, and would probably be there more than a week as my condition was critical.

Blood transfusion? Of all the things I was told, those words kept echoing in my head. It freaked me out, to say the least. I now had somebody else's blood in me! That was a very, very weird, creepy feeling and hard to describe. I understood that the blood transfusion saved my life, because I almost bled to death from the ruptured spleen, but it was still a very unusual and awkward concept to grasp. I felt relieved to know there was a blood match, but more concerned to discover I had another person's blood in my system. The weird, creepy feeling definitely outweighed the relieved feeling; that was going to take a while to digest. He did not say anything about being paralyzed. Either I wasn't or he failed to mention that part.

"So," the surgeon said as he continued explaining my condition, "you have a chest tube in under your left arm to drain the fluid from around your lung so we can get that lung to re-inflate. There was a lot of blood and fluid in there from the trauma; your ribs literally penetrated and punctured your left lung. You will be in a lot of pain from your ribs, from the chest tube, and the incision on your stomach. We may even have to plate a few of your ribs, as you crushed four of them pretty badly." *"I" crushed them? Like I did this to myself? The ribs just broke, I didn't break them.*

He pointed to my fractured ribs on the x-ray and showed me a plastic rib plate. As a hygienist, I have seen broken bones on x-rays, so I could recognize my broken ribs right way. However, it did not take an expert to notice that they were very badly displaced and looked like a mess. They were pointing in every direction: some up, some down, some in, some out. It looked more like a pile of bare, baby back rib bones on a plate instead of my protective rib cage.

"You have a pretty good-size incision down your belly where they cut you open to remove your spleen," the surgeon continued.

"Really? The surgeon at Woodland Park said it would be a few inches," I said. Wow, this news was going from bad to worse. I couldn't wait to hear what else. However, I was grateful to be alive. And he still had not mentioned anything about paralysis.

"Oh, this is more than a few inches. Have you looked at it yet?" he asked.

"No," I said. "Can't wait."

"When you're ready to look at it, let me know. I'll be here with you," he stated. "They couldn't do it laparoscopically because it was badly ruptured; in fact, it pretty much blew up (*Wow, this guy doesn't sugar coat anything*).

They had to remove all your organs to see what was damaged, what was bleeding, and get you cleaned up because there was a lot of internal bleeding." He could tell I was trying to absorb all this information; he let that sink in then he told me, "The surgeon and his team in Woodland Park said if you had arrived fifteen minutes later, you wouldn't be here with us today. You were pretty banged up and lost a lot of blood from your spleen rupture. It's a good thing you stopped there that day."

"Oh," he said, "And the surgeon who was there, he wasn't even on duty. He just happened to stop by on his way home from town. Somebody was looking out for you that day!"

But wait; they said a couple of ribs. I had eight broken ribs! That's almost all of them on one side! Thoughts of anatomy class and a hanging skeleton popped into my mind. I heard him continue, "We may have to plate some of those ribs, which would entail another surgery, a pretty invasive surgery. We would have to expose those ribs to put this plastic plate on them." He waved the plastic rib he held in his hand. "We would make an incision from the middle of your chest under your arm and into the middle of your back to expose the broken ribs, screw this plastic plate on, and stitch you back up. I have seen patients who I would say definitely need them plated, and I have seen patients who shouldn't have them plated." He told me I was right in the middle; I could go either way.

"Let's see how you do over the next few days, then we'll decide. You're going to be here over a week, if not more, so we have plenty of time to think about it," he said.

A WEEK! Holy crap, a week? Those words stung. I could not believe my ears. I thought I'd be out of there in a few more days. I just told my sister I wouldn't be there long. Again, my mind went back to, "There's just no way this has happened; there's no way." I was not willing to believe it at all. My mind was all over the place. I had so many thoughts I could not even focus on one. I had a blood transfusion, broken ribs, punctured lung, hospital stay over a week, huge scar on my belly! It was amazing to me how many thoughts could be going on at once and I was not able to focus on a single one. I was like the kid in the candy store who wants all the candy he or she sees and needs to concentrate on just one. I had to stop the downward spiral and gather my positive thoughts. *I was not paralyzed, and I was alive!*

I did see my boys as I went in and out of sleep. We were just hanging out doing absolutely nothing. We tried to watch TV and have conversations, but I could tell they were upset and felt horrible for me. I could still see the concern in their eyes. I wished they wouldn't worry, but I knew they were deeply concerned. I tried to reassure them I would be OK. I felt horrible and guilty for the hurt I saw on their faces. I didn't want to cause them any grief; I didn't like hurting people and I definitely didn't like being a bother to people.

As a parent one of the worst things in the world is to see your kids hurt, whether it's physical or emotional. I never understood this feeling until I had children of my own. I experienced my first heartbreak at the age of sixteen, when I discovered my first "real boyfriend," my true love, had cheated on me with another girl. I was devastated and pretty much thought my life was over. I had little to no desire to do anything; I just cried and cried, during the day, during the night. My heart and my stomach hurt so much I thought it was going to explode. My mom tried to console me, but it did not help, no offense to her. It was one of the few times she did try to help in that way. She told me there were other fish in the sea, but I didn't want other fish; I wanted that fish. I wanted Jack. My mother tried to explain to me that it hurt her to see me hurt. I had no idea what she was talking about and thought she was a little crazy. How could she be hurt? This was my hurt, my heartache. After I had children of my own, I understood this concept completely. It hurts so much to see my kids hurt; it makes my heart literally ache.

Not only was my heart broken, but my head hurt from thinking, *Why, why, did Jack do this to me?* I needed to understand why he cheated on me, why I wasn't good enough, why he didn't want me anymore, what she had that I didn't, and what was wrong with me. I had never felt this kind of pain and confusion before, and I knew I didn't want to feel it again, EVER. It was the worst my heart had ever hurt; in all of my sixteen years that was the worst emotional pain I had ever experienced. I wondered if my heart would ever heal. Did I mention, I do not like pain? Physical or mental?

I was glad my boys and Matt were all there. I was scared, scared to death, as they say—hopefully, not literally. I did not want my boys to know that I was frightened. I needed to be strong for them. I needed to be there for them to cushion their hurt, to support them. I needed to let them know I was going to be OK, but deep down I was a wreck. I had never been so scared in my entire life. I wondered if I was going to die, literally, die. That was not just a figure of speech; that feeling was real. *Was I going to be my normal self again? Was I going to be in pain for the rest of my life? Would I be able to walk? Would I be able to lift weights and compete again?*

As the week went on, I remained in the ICU but was getting better. At least I thought I was doing better. It seemed like a slow process, but I was so grateful to be alive. I thought of others who have been in ATV accidents who have not been as fortunate as we were. I have heard several stories of people who died, had brain damage, or paralysis. *Wow, we were really lucky—or were we?*

Luck was not something I had much of. Good things did not happen to me. My life as a child was all about survival; luck wasn't part of that. I felt other people were "lucky" because their parents were involved with their lives; they were "lucky" because their parents came to their school events; they were "lucky" because their moms came into the classrooms to help; they were "lucky" because their parents and families loved them; they were "lucky" because their boyfriends didn't cheat on them. My needs, basic needs, were always taken care of. I had a roof over my head, food, clean clothes, and a nice bed. I wanted the love, the support, the confidence, the self-esteem. I wanted to feel important. I wanted to matter to someone. I wanted to be someone's everything.

The nurses in ICU were amazing. They took care of me, helped me, talked with me, and reassured all of us that I was going to be OK and that the worst of it was definitely over. It made me feel good to know they cared.

My whole life I have been starving for people to care for and love me, really care for and love me. People say those words and throw them around loosely, but I'm talking about deep-down love and care. For most of my life I felt alone and thought nobody was there for me. Whether that's how it truly was or just my perception, I felt alone, unsafe, and insecure. My parents were good at providing my basic needs but, unfortunately, not good at making me feel loved. I firmly believe they did the best they could; it just wasn't what I wanted or needed. It wasn't the love and comfort I needed to make me feel safe, secure, or confident. I continue to search for that place where I feel totally loved. I want to be important to someone.

I remember vividly when the medical staff made me stand for the first time after the surgery. It was amazing to me that as a former gymnast and fitness competitor, I needed help to stand up. *Really? Holy cow, what have I done to my body? It must be pretty banged up.* For the first time in my life, standing was a challenge. I had very little strength, but I did have drive and determination to stand and walk again. The thought of fitness competing was out the window at that point. Stepping on stage with a two-minute routine where strength and flexibility were displayed was not even something my brain could comprehend. It made me sad to think I might never do a one-arm push-up again. *WHOA, slow down, baby steps,* I kept telling myself. *Baby steps. Let's walk and get out of the hospital first.* I had to stay focused on the present and not think about the future just yet. The future made me sad, frustrated, and scared.

My legs and body were shaking from lack of strength and fear. It had been several days since I had been upright, and I could not believe I was scared to stand. I stood with a lot of assistance; my ICU nurse, the physical therapist, and the occupational therapist were all firmly holding onto me as best they could. The ICU nurse slowly released my arm, the physical therapist released me, and finally the occupational therapist released me. I wasn't sure if I was more surprised than they were that I did not fall down. But there I was, standing on my own. *Whooo Whooo, I did it. I'm standing up.* I was weak, but I was standing, not totally upright, but I was standing!

Now the physical therapist wanted me to march in place. *Is he kidding?* I couldn't even move my left side, and he wanted me to lift my feet up off the floor? My right leg did much better than my left. I could barely raise my left leg. I did manage to pick up my foot a little, but not enough to get my foot entirely off the floor. It was a major reality slap in the face to me. I could barely walk. *Are you kidding me? I can't even lift my foot up off the floor!* It made me realize for the first time how bad I was. How badly hurt I was physically. I knew they kept telling me of my injuries, but I didn't think it would be THAT bad. I was devastated, disappointed, and mostly scared that I would never be the same physically active self. *I ride ATVs, I wakeboard, I snowboard, I compete in body building, I lift weights, I need my physical ability back and I want it now!!!* I was on the verge of hysterics as tears streamed down my face.

"You'll get there," the PT said. "Keep marching."

I attempted to march for what seemed like forty-five minutes, but it was only four or five minutes. I lay back down with a lot of help and, boy, was I exhausted and frustrated. *Time for me to rest.*

My mind raced: I was going to be OK, I was never going to be the same, I wanted to go home, and I wanted to stay there in ICU where they could take care of me. I was brave, I was scared, I was concerned, I was relieved, I was thankful, I was pissed, I was strong, and I was weak. I guess it was safe to say, I was an emotional wreck. What a roller coaster ride. I usually like roller coasters, but not this mental one I was on. I wanted off. I wanted this ride to be over! I wanted to be better NOW. I wanted to walk, to run, to go lift weights.

I told my boys and Matt, "I'm going to take a quick nap now." They took this opportunity to go get something to eat. I wondered if they even had an appetite. I know I didn't. I felt they were afraid to leave me, but I was going to be OK, I kept telling them. After they left, I did a lot of quiet praying while I lay there and felt very grateful they were there for me.

Matt and my boys had a good relationship. They were not extremely close but got along fine, probably even enjoyed each other's company a little at times. Matt is an only child and pretty much grew up doing whatever he wanted whenever he wanted. He was raised in Cheyenne, Wyoming, and Summit County, Colorado. His mom tried to discipline him as any mother would, but I have a feeling she had her work cut out for her. Matt is a very hard worker with a phenomenal work ethic, something I admire in him. He is responsible with money and bills and extremely smart beyond his years, all of which I also find attractive.

After I woke up from my nap, the nurses told me I had to start walking. *Walking?* Again, I was strong and weak, and I was brave and scared at the same time. We were making progress. "We" as in my team there: the nurses, my boys, my boyfriend, and all my fluids, my IVs, my chest tube, and my higher power and angels. I was definitely a package deal. I stood still forever as they unhooked, re-hooked, and rearranged all the cords, tubes, and carts needed for that journey. *Where was my pain med pump? Need that, must have that.* My boyfriend grabbed a chair in case I needed to rest on my walk. "My walk," they said. We were talking halfway down the hall, which was all of 15 feet, I believe. Halfway down the hall was a long way away for me.

"Are you up for it?" the nurse asked.

"Yep, let's do this," I said. "I'm ready!" It was up to me now.

We started our journey going out the ICU room. My right leg stepped and my left leg just kind of dragged. I never realized how many back muscles are required to lift your leg. *Come on body*, I told myself. *You can do this; you can walk.* It hurt like hell, yes, but no pain, no gain. *Keep going. You're almost there. You're gonna make it.* I was pretty good at the self-pep talks.

I made it to my goal destination, and we turned around. Wow, my body was so messed up I could hardly walk, but I was determined to heal and get better. There's that damn roller coaster ride again: *I'm not ever going to be the same. I was so strong. I'm so scared. I'm so determined. I want to give up. I can do this; no, I can't.* My mind brought me back to reality. I just had to focus on staying upright to get back to my bed. Matt followed close with the chair, but I was too stubborn to admit I needed to rest and use it. *Really, Diane? It is only a few feet away and you need to stop? Yeah, you need to stop—stop being a sissy; get your body moving and keep going. You can do this.*

Yahooooo, I did it; I made it. I didn't lay back down right away. I had to sit upright in a chair for a few minutes before I could go back to bed. *Ugh, when do I get to rest?*

"Let's shoot for ten minutes in the chair, OK?" one of the nurses asked.

"Of course, I can do ten minutes," I said.

It felt so good to sit upright, but I DID NOT want to sit all the way back in the chair. I didn't want anything touching my back. It was so painful. I cannot even begin to tell you the pain I experienced from my ribs. *When will that pain go away*, I wondered? *It's been several days.* The surgeon even put an anesthetic catheter in my back to keep it numb to help with the pain. I wondered if it was even working, as my back hurt beyond belief. They had it cranked all the way up so the anesthetic was flowing as fast as it could. Even though I do not like pain, I have a pretty high pain tolerance and am tough when dealing with pain. Usually I heal quickly, but this seemed to be taking forever.

I had an amazing respiratory therapist working with me, but I dreaded every time she came in. I had breathing exercises to do for my lungs. I had to use a spirometer, where you blow out all of your air and suck it back in through that plastic machine. It measures how much air you are getting. My goal was 1,000, but I was barely getting 200. The pain in my back and chest was so incredible, I could not fully inhale or exhale. But I knew this was important and knew pain was necessary to heal and get better, so I tried hard. I gave it all I had. *I will get there. I know I will.*

I had another flutter thing I had to blow into. I had to take a deep breath and blow out until I couldn't blow out anymore. I never realized breathing could be so painful. There were times I didn't think I was going to survive it, I was in so much pain. I wanted to cry and scream at the top of my lungs. *Oh, but wait; that will hurt!* I tried hard to be strong and not let my family know how much I hurt, how scared I was. I needed to be strong.

"Be tough, be strong" was something I heard over and over during my childhood. My parents said it, and my siblings said it. Strong was an adjective instilled in my conscious and subconscious mind. Strong can refer to physical status, but my family used it figuratively. Mentally, be strong, be tough. Emotionally, be strong, be tough. I firmly believe they thought if you're tough and strong, you are a good person, you'll survive, and you'll make it. We were not taught how to deal with feelings and emotions; we were just told to be strong. That might have been a way to hide what we were really feeling. Or maybe acting tough showed people we were strong, and we could handle a situation.

I am so grateful Matt was with me during my stay in the hospital. I did not want to be alone. After much persuasion, we convinced my boys to head back home. I reassured them they would be of more help at home taking care of the dogs than sitting there with me. There was nothing they could do at the hospital but worry. I actually did want them to stay and be with me, but I also wanted to spare them the pain of seeing me like this. There was snow in the forecast, and someone needed to be with the dogs; it made sense to send them home. I did not want my boys driving back and forth from Colorado Springs to Denver in the snow on Interstate 25 up over Monument Hill. Monument Hill is about 7,000 feet in elevation between the two cities where road conditions and traffic can be treacherous. My boys were reluctant to leave but finally decided to go. I was scared to say goodbye for fear I would not wake up tomorrow, but I was grateful they would be safe at home.

Matt and I talked about plating the ribs. As with any decision, there were pros and cons. The doctor said I would probably be fine without plating, and I really, really, really did not want another surgery, and a very invasive surgery at that. Unfortunately, Matt was not much help as he said it was entirely up to me. I decided not to do the plating. It wasn't just the surgery I dreaded so much but that tube down my throat! Yikes. I don't ever want to experience that tube again.

After seven days in ICU, they decided I was fine to

go to a "regular room." I was sad to leave. I had gotten to know the nurses and therapists in there, and they were ALL so awesome. They catered to my every medical need, and I trusted them. One amazing nurse even gave my boyfriend a better chair to sleep in and found him a place to take a shower. I was going to miss them.

The next few days were pretty boring as I lay there and continued my recovery. I still got visits from my team—physical therapists, an occupational therapist, respiratory therapist, nurses, doctors, surgeons, and radiology techs. The visits were not as frequent as they were in ICU, but I was OK with that; it meant I was getting better. I was told I would get to go home when the fluid was drained from around my lung. Believe me, watching the fluid drain did not make it go any faster. Kind of like the watched pot never boils. We just waited as patiently as possible.

Patience has never been one of my strong characteristics. It is a standing joke with my family that I had NO patience at all. I wanted everything yesterday, and I am guilty of wanting instant gratification in most areas of my life. After some maturing, I realized instant results aren't always possible; just seeing progress, even if small, was very inspiring. Over the years, my sister Lynn has taught me it was God's time, not my time. Still to this day when I get in a hurry or stressed about instant results, I hear Lynn's words going through my mind.

Going Home

*"Faith is taking the first step even when you
don't see the whole staircase."*

—MARTIN LUTHER KING JR.

FINALLY, THE DAY CAME, and I got to go home. We
had been watching the weather for a couple days, and
they were predicting a snowstorm. Colorado Springs is
about 70 miles from home for us, but we had to travel
up and over Monument Hill. There was a part of me
that wanted to stay. *What if we get into an accident? What
if we go in the ditch? What if the highway was closed?* I
didn't know how to take care of myself yet, I didn't
have the proper supplies. I was just short of going into
panic mode. I was scared of leaving the hospital, but I
did want to be home.

After I realized driving home was inevitable, it was time to put on my big girl panties and be brave. We asked the hospital team if we could get out of there as early as possible that morning, and they were awesome at the releasing procedure. I started to get excited to go home, but reality kicked in again. *I am so scared to leave. I don't know how to take care of myself yet. I am still in so much pain. What if I take a turn for the worse no one's there to take care of me? What am I going to do?*

Reluctantly, I climbed into the car. It was cold, it was snowing, and I was extremely nervous. I was a wreck on the drive (no pun intended). It seemed like hours, and the roads were snowy and icy, but we made it home safe and sound before the big snow. I'm sure Matt was nervous on the drive also, but he drove very carefully. I was definitely relieved yet still scared at the same time—very mixed feelings. I thought the emotional roller coaster was over ... guess not! I was grateful to be home; it seemed like it had been forever since I had been there. The nurses at the hospital had done an amazing job, and I knew there was no way I could do the same. I was so hurt, so damaged, and in so much pain. I could barely walk (but was very grateful I was not paralyzed).

I had 24-hour supervision at home for the first several days. Between my boyfriend, my boys, and my sister, I was not left alone. We set up a bed for me in the living room on the couch part of our sectional where Matt, Matthew, and Hunter took turns sleeping with me. I thanked God for them many times, because I was so scared to be alone. I was afraid I was going to fall asleep and not wake up. I would lie there at night just short of freaking out with fear: fear of the unknown, fear of my future, fear of dying. Nobody knew how panicked inside I really was.

Being alone freaked me out when I was younger, even sometimes as an adult. I hated being alone physically, but emotionally I loathed being alone, because it frightened me. For the majority of my life, I had no self-esteem, no comfort, and no confidence; I felt empty, scared, and lonely. I had no one there for me. On Sunday evenings I became so concerned about having to go to school on Mondays because I had to go alone that I worried myself sick, literally ill. I hated that insecure, empty feeling more than anything. Abandoned by everyone, abandoned by myself.

Lynn came over every day for my first week home to stay with me. Matt and Matthew had to go back to work, and Hunter had to go to school and finish his senior year in high school.

Lynn, who's been like a mom to me, easily stepped into her role of helping me. She never had any children of her own. I never understood God's plan for her, as she is an amazing woman and would have been a great mom. Her children have been four-legged, furry ones. She took a week vacation from work to come stay with me during the day, driving forty-five minutes to an hour

in snow every day. I was so very grateful she came over.
I was scared to be alone still. It had only been two weeks
since the accident, but it was my first week home, and I
still needed help getting up, walking, using the restroom,
and pretty much everything else. I needed the company
physically, but mostly mentally and emotionally.

Over the next several weeks I had many follow-up
doctor's visits with CAT scans, only to discover more
bad news. I had fluid around my lung that might need
to be removed because my lung was not re-inflating,
which meant either another surgery or another chest
tube. I had fluid around my heart as well that might
need to be removed because it could interfere with my
heart function. The chest pain I still experienced was
from a pneumothorax (air pocket), and I had two more
broken ribs on the front right side. My liver also was
badly bruised, but no treatment was recommended for
that. *What the heck was going on? Every time I turn around
it's something else. I am never going to get better.*

Emotional Roller Coaster

"Being negative only makes a difficult journey more difficult."

—JOYCE MEYER

AS THE DAYS WENT BY, my mind teetered back and forth between feelings of reassurance that I was going to be OK and feeling there was no way I was going to be OK. My mind did not know what to think; my body had never been in this situation before. My body had never been this messed up, this broken, this dysfunctional. I usually am a very positive person and can find the good in anything, but some moments then that was hard to do, almost impossible at times.

Over the next several weeks, I did continue to get better, very slowly in my opinion. Very slowly, but at least I made progress and didn't regress any further. As an athlete, I wanted my body to heal and to heal quickly; even yesterday wasn't soon enough. I have never expected something for nothing. I am willing to put in the work and put forth the effort, but I do want to see results, noticeable results.

I now had several hours in my days that I was left alone and could manage a few basic functions, not many but enough to be left alone. My family and friends had been so good at helping me. I felt very grateful I had such an awesome support system.

My boyfriend and two boys had been there as much as they could. They shared responsibilities of shoveling snow, cooking dinner, going to the store, and doing household chores. On Matt's first trip to the grocery store he spent about $500. He wanted to make sure we had enough food, as we had people coming and going a lot. I am not sure what he was thinking, but I sure thought it was sweet.

I felt totally helpless, like a failure. I could not even make Matt a cup of coffee in the mornings or my boys a cup of hot chocolate before work and school. I love doing that simple chore; it is by far one of my favorite things to do for my family. I do not know why that one is so fulfilling to me, but it is. I guess drinking a cup of coffee or hot chocolate with my loved ones is true bonding time for me. It always felt very rewarding. It was one of those small things in life I am grateful for that I now couldn't fulfill. What a loser, what a failure.

I tried to remind myself of the things I should be grateful for, like walking and normal brain function. But! There was a big but! I could tell I was not right. I was not my normal positive self. My thinking was not where it should be, and I was very aware of that. I was so stressed about getting back to normal that I could not even relax. I wanted to be better NOW. I tried reading, I tried watching positive videos on YouTube, and I tried feeding my mind with good, positive, uplifting thoughts. I knew I needed to take that time to breathe, relax, and heal my mind and my body, but it wasn't happening that way. I told myself over and over to be patient, to take advantage of the down time, and use the quiet time to my advantage.

I could not seem to focus on what I was reading or watching, so there I sat and just stared at the TV. Watching daytime television was definitely not in my best interest. Need I say more how depressing that was? I was normally not home during the day like that, and there I was, day after day, hour after hour, watching nothing but bad news and crazy talk shows that only made me further depressed. I think I watched every episode there was of *Family Feud*. I thought every negative thought I could wrap my brain around. I felt every negative feeling I could come up with. I was feeling so sorry for myself. I cannot even put into words how sorry. It was crazy. I kept wondering what was happening to me, what was going on. I was thinking thoughts I had never had before, but I never had any suicidal thoughts; hell, I was trying to survive.

I was frustrated with everything. People in general, my doctors, my family, my employer, my boyfriend, the TV, and, of course, myself—mostly myself. Isn't that the way it works? Isn't anger one of the steps in the grieving process? Well, I hit the anger stage. It seemed I was mad at everything. I was pissed off at Matt for not cuddling me, for not loving me the way I wanted him to, for not holding me, for not telling me he loved me, for not reassuring me everything was going to be OK, for not paying attention to me. Me, me, me! I wanted the world to stop a minute and grieve with me, to show their empathy for me, to make me feel important and special. I was so scared, and I wanted Matt to make it all better. I put a lot of weight on him, holding him responsible for me getting better, for making me happy, and making sure everything was going to be OK.

Looking back, I know he was doing his best. He did his share to help and be there, but it was not what I had imagined; it was not the way I wanted it to be. I would ask him to sit next to me on the couch. I would ask him to hold me, and he would say he couldn't because I was hurt. I thought he was avoiding me. I thought he did not love me because I was broken, because I had an ugly 12-inch scar that ran down my belly, because I had a hole in the side of my chest. I don't know what it was, but it made me angry, it made me sad, and it made me feel completely unlovable, unworthy, and, once again in my life, unimportant and a nobody. *He doesn't even care about me.* Then the sad, negative downward spiral would begin to swirl in my head again, leaving me to feel sorry for myself even more. I was looking for anything and everything negative I could find, trying to convince myself I was not lovable. After all, how could anyone love me? I was broken. I knew my kids and my family loved me; they are family and are supposed to love me. But all I was after was Matt's love and acceptance at this point; for some reason that was all that mattered.

During this time, Matt helped me financially because I was out of work awhile. He did more than his share around the house, but I didn't care if he did the dishes, or went to the store, or shoveled snow; I wanted his love and attention. I greatly appreciated all those things, but I wanted him. I wanted him to feel sorry for me, I wanted him to cry with me, and I wanted him to feel the pain I was feeling. I wanted his undivided attention; I wanted to feel his love. I wanted to know he loved me. I wanted him to care in the ways I wanted him to care. I wanted to know he would still accept me even if I was broken. He always said whatever he does was not good enough, but that was not true in my head or my mind. I just wanted his love, and I wanted to be treated with love and respect. He does a lot of nice things for us, but I wanted to be treated the way I want. It's not as if those other things go unnoticed; it's just they're not as important to me as his love and attention. That is all I wanted — love and attention. I wanted him to be compassionate and caring.

I didn't really know what was going on in his head or his world; all I knew was what was going on in mine. And it wasn't pretty; it wasn't good. I sat there day after day, hour after hour, convincing myself he did not care, that he did not love me, that he only stuck around because he felt sorry for me. That only drove the hurt deeper into my chest. My chest already hurt, but this was different; this was true heartache not just chest pain from the broken ribs or collapsed lung. My heart hurt, and my body craved love and attention.

I kept thinking he had to be struggling with all of this, too. Surely, he had to be; he had been driving. I cannot even begin to imagine what he must have been feeling or thinking. I was not mad at him for the crash or for my broken body. I had not blamed him for any part of it — never have and never will. When you are active, there are usually injuries of some sort. But I never even once, not even for a split second, blamed him for this accident. He was driving but was not being careless or engaging in any dangerous activity. He was not drinking alcohol or driving stupid. It was purely an accident. I'm sure he felt bad, felt responsible, but I wasn't holding him responsible; why was he holding himself responsible? Or was he? Was he mad at himself? Was he mad at me? I couldn't tell what was going on and communicating was not an option at that point. We didn't discuss the accident or my health much. It was a sore subject (no pun intended). I couldn't even figure out my own head. I knew I shouldn't even try to get into his.

Matt also suffered injuries, but he was so fortunate they weren't worse, as he was not wearing a helmet that day. His left forearm was solid road rash, with red, raw skin and gravel pieces embedded in the open wounds. His left hip was very badly bruised, and that eventually spread over his entire left thigh. It was the worst bruise I have ever seen, and I am not exaggerating when I say his entire quadricep and left buttock were a discolored very, very, deep red, purple, and even black.

I felt like we were drifting further and further apart. On several occasions I tried to talk to him, but I could tell he did not want to keep rehashing it. I wanted to know what had happened and how we had crashed. Did I land on him on the ground? Did the ATV roll on me? I did not ask how fast we were going. I was looking for answers; I was not looking for blame. I am a big "why" person, and I felt the need to understand how we crashed and why. Not to place fault, but for my own understanding. I felt if I knew this, I could heal better and faster. I just wanted to know what had happened.

I have read stories of tragic things happening to families and ripping them totally apart. *Wow, could this be happening to us? Was our relationship going to survive?*

Matt and I had a unique complicated relationship, difficult at times. We were not always on the same page or even in the same book. It's like we were in some sort of competition. I have no idea what we were competing for, but some days it was indeed a battle. We had been living together for six months prior to the accident and had traveled a fairly rocky road to say the least (no pun intended). We almost split up in December prior to our February mishap.

In my world of relationships, we should have been growing closer together, not tearing apart. The accident was something tragic, major, literally life changing. We were there together just the two of us during that tragedy; we should be bonding. Now on top of everything else I was afraid I was going to lose my boyfriend. I was feeling so alone and insecure, and this caused me to cling more, which only made matters worse. The more love and attention I ached for, the more I expressed my concerns and insecurities. *There goes my mind again, and the feelings, and the chest pain. Wait, I think that chest pain was physical from the collapsed lung, not emotional. Ugh. I can't tell anymore. I'm going to take a nap.* Lynn used to tell me just go to sleep when something was bothering me. *Well, I am definitely bothered — time to nap.*

When I woke up, the pain, the feelings, the thoughts were all still right where I left them. My body and mind were confused, physically, mentally, and spiritually. I had to remind myself to be patient and take one step at a time. Those answers would come in time. I started to pray, talked out loud, even screamed. I yearned for direction from anyone or anything that would listen to my cries and lead me to a path of recovery with a positive attitude.

Everything Happens for a Reason

*"Sometimes when things are falling apart, they
may actually be falling into place."*

—A COURAGEOUS PERSON

MY SISTER JANET IS THREE YEARS OLDER than I am,
and we had a typical sister relationship growing up. I
followed her everywhere, tried wearing her clothes, and
pretty much drove her crazy. She used to get so mad at
me for wanting to do everything she did and be with
her constantly. I even followed her to the hayloft with
my cousins where they learned to smoke. I still give her
grief to this day for taking me with them. Of course,
when you're nine years old, you don't make the best
decisions. Most of our childhood we shared a bedroom
and even a bed. We were super close physically, but

emotionally seemed to teeter on and off. At one point in my life, I felt closer to her than anyone else. I knew she would always be there for me, NO MATTER WHAT. Even though I may not feel as close to her as I maybe do to Lynn, I know Janet will always be there for me. She had her part in helping raise me as well.

She is a pharmacy tech, and I reached out to her on several occasions about the drugs I had taken, the side effects, and my blood transfusion. She used to work at Bonfils Blood Center and knew I was still freaked out about my transfusion. I had tons of questions. For those who know me, that was not shocking, as I have a reputation for questioning everything.

Even though all my siblings did not have a significant role in my recovery, I would like to mention them. My oldest brother, Joe, resides in Iowa and is fifteen years older than I am. He and I were not close at all growing up. I believe most of that was because of the age difference. I remember writing letters back and forth to him while he was in Vietnam when I was four. He got married and moved out of the house when I was little, so I do not even remember him being at home. Tom is my second oldest brother, and we didn't know each other much growing up either. I have gotten to know him better as we aged. He is thirteen years older than I am and moved out when I was little; he lives in Texas. Ann is the oldest girl in my family and is twelve years older than I am. She helped raised me while our mom worked her three jobs. Ann and I have never been super close but would be there for each other in a heartbeat. She lives in Colorado. Lynn is the next in line. As I've said, she and I are extremely close, and she had a huge impact on my recovery and my life. Danny is the youngest boy, seven years older than I am. He and I talk off and on, sometimes more on than off. He resides in Colorado as well. We, too, seem closer at times than others. I really enjoy our conversations and value his opinion.

I love all my siblings dearly with all my heart. I am grateful we have remained in contact but do wish we were a little closer emotionally and physically. Each and every one of them had some sort of impact on my upbringing, so I would like to thank them for their part in shaping who I have become.

I tried to brainstorm with Janet about what happened to me and why. Crashes were part of our childhood, but this one was different. I wanted to figure out how I crashed, what I landed on, whether the ATV crushed me, and whether I landed on Matt or he landed on me. Maybe she could help me determine what happened. But she told me, "You're just going to have to accept you were in an accident and move on. It does not matter why; it does not matter how. Accept it, let it go, and move on." Those words stung me and replayed over and over in my head for days, weeks, and even years now. She was absolutely right: accept it, let it go, and move on. Unfortunately, it was way easier said than done, but it did help me tremendously with my healing process. Whenever I got into my funk and beat myself up about what happened, I would take a minute to just accept it. Yes, I was in an accident, I was very broken, I was never going to be the same, but it was OK. It happened, embrace it, and move on. Breathe in, breathe out.

Matt told me the same thing when I tried troubleshooting with him. "Fuck Diane, we were in an accident; let it go. It's over, it's done, let it go." But I couldn't. I had to know what happened that day in Divide on Road 364. It had been about two-and-a-half weeks since that tragic event, and I still couldn't or didn't want to stop obsessing over what and why.

I had those ATVs for seven years, and I rode that road many times, going over that jump many times. *Why was it different that time? Why did we crash?* I continued to unravel the mishap in my mind and out loud over the next few days. I repeated the words "accept it" over and over, first in my head, then out loud until I screamed it at the top of my lungs. Suddenly, it hit me like a lightning bolt—"accept it." It resonated with me big time. I got it, I felt it. Up to that point I had not accepted it. I was still fighting it. I was still in denial. I decided right then and there to accept it. I decided to quit boycotting the fact that I had been in a tragic, almost fatal ATV accident.

I started looking into the grieving process. I needed to grieve and move on. How does one grieve? How does that work? I felt I truly did not know how to grieve. It was not something I was taught or ever experienced. I thought grieving was something you did when someone died. I did not realize you could grieve an accident or an event in your life. For the first time in weeks, I was excited for something. I was excited to do some research. I liked learning.

I am a firm believer that everything does happen for a reason. My boys and I have lived by this mantra for years. I am not exactly sure how that saying became so important to us, but it did. Countless times we would be bummed out or disappointed that something didn't happen the way we thought it should, only later to find out it wasn't supposed to happen the way we wanted. Sometimes the reason came out right away or within a few days and, of course, for some things we're still waiting for the reason.

What about the accident? Why did this happen to me, to us? What was the reason? I didn't know the answers, but I was convinced there was a purpose and it would be revealed someday.

I could not rely on anyone, I could not trust anyone, and I had no faith, no belief in anyone or myself. I was all alone.

In *You Can Heal Your Life,* author Louise Hay writes that accidents can be caused from pent-up anger. *Wow, I guess I had pent-up anger, and a lot of it.* And I was not real sure where all that anger was stemming from, but I did know I was angry with myself more than anyone or anything else, and I had been angry for a long time. I knew I was responsible for my feelings and I was mad at myself. *Shouldn't I be able to change my feelings, my thoughts? Just feel better, just feel happy. Ha! That was easy.* That thought only lasted a split second, but it was a start. I needed to figure out my feelings, how to control my feelings and thoughts instead of letting them control me. I needed to learn how to change my thoughts. I needed to learn a lot of things about myself. I needed to get to know who I really was. First on the list, I wanted to know how to let things go. That thought of needing to know why and how the accident happened was killing me. *Literally, this is going to kill me if I don't fix it.*

Growing up we were quick to anger. That seemed our first response, especially to pain. When we were hurt, we got angry. When we were frustrated, we got angry. Even though anger was expressed in several circumstances, it was never out of control; it was used as a normal emotion around my house, and it was used often.

Matt, my boys, and my family were all amazing at helping and taking care of me during this ordeal, but there was still something missing. It was ME. I was missing. My recovery or happiness was not in their hands. It was up to me and my Divine Team (Thanks, Tonja Waring, author of *Single Mom on Fire*, for teaching me about my Divine Team). My Divine Team consisted of me, my higher power, my angels, and the universe—my team! I was always a team player, so this was going to be fun. I had a team, I belonged, and I was an important player in this new game.

I do believe there is a God, but I also question it from time to time because I cannot physically see Him. As I mentioned, for the most part I have to see to believe. Lynn continues to help me with my "faith" and tells me I am a work in progress. I do believe I am getting better.

I wanted to love myself, I wanted comfort, I wanted confidence, I wanted security, I wanted positive reassurance, and I wanted to matter. I wanted somebody to be there for me, be there in the way I wanted, be there in the way I needed. After relentless hours of diving deep into my soul, my head, and my heart about what I wanted, I finally realized I needed to go within and get what I desired, because I was not getting those needs met from the outside. Give all those things to myself; give to myself as I would give to someone else. Be there for myself as I would for someone I loved. Love myself the way I would love someone else. *Holy cow, this is a MAJOR aha moment for me. Do I hear myself correctly? Go within! Go get what I want from myself and treat myself like I want to be treated. Love myself the way I want to be loved.* I was certainly onto something big and wonderful.

In all my fifty years, that thought had never existed, but it was so perfect for my life. That was exactly what I needed to hear, to think, and to feel. Turn within to myself for what I want and need. Love me!

Letting Go

"You are confined only by the walls you build around yourself."

—ANDREW MURPHY

TO SAY I WAS ON A MISSION was an understatement. I knew my course, and I knew it was going to be amazing. I felt peaceful and relieved for the first time in weeks. I finally understood why I was in an ATV accident. That accident was a wakeup call for me. It happened in order to teach me how to love and respect myself, finally, after all these years. I have learned how to accept myself for who I am. My purpose is then to teach others how to love and respect themselves. Help others build self-esteem and live to their full potential by first loving and respecting themselves. Profound!

Respect was something we grew up with, but not much emphasis on respecting ourselves. We were taught to respect authority, people older than we were, our teachers, and our family, but not ourselves. It was as if we treated other people better than ourselves. I'm not sure if this was our family values or Catholic education, but that's what we did; we put everybody else first. It wasn't right to be selfish. I understand this concept a little differently now. I do think it is appropriate to put people first and do for them first, but we must love and respect ourselves initially along the way. Love ourselves so we can love others.

First, I had to let go of the anger I was holding. I had so much anger inside at my mom, my family, my boyfriend, my job, my network marketing business, my entire life, and, of course, myself. I did not know how to relieve my anger and how to forgive people. I had always struggled with forgiving and letting go, ever since I could remember. To me, forgiving meant it was OK for the things that happened to have happened. If I forgave someone, in my mind that meant, "You can treat me like that again." Or maybe I could forgive, but I could never forget. I would hold a grudge full of anger and just wait for it to happen again. I was horrible at forgiving others, so the concept of forgiving myself wasn't even fathomable. It never even occurred to me to forgive myself. But this was where I felt I needed to start. If I was going to treat myself like a person I greatly cared for, learning how to love and respect myself was definitely what I needed to learn.

I knew I needed to forgive everyone in my outside world for not treating me THE WAY I WANTED TO BE TREATED. But mostly, I had to forgive myself for not treating myself better all those years, and especially right now. I needed to forgive myself for not standing up for myself all those times and allowing bad things to happen. I needed to forgive myself for not speaking out. I needed to forgive myself for being ignorant and not protecting myself.

I allowed my grandfather to sexually abuse me when I was ten. I never stopped him. I didn't have enough self-confidence to say stop. I didn't think enough of myself to put him in his place. I didn't love myself enough to protect my body. I didn't have the power to say no. I was a meek, shy, insecure, defenseless little girl. I didn't talk about this outside of counseling much because I believed it was my fault that he did it. I must have done something wrong. I must have warranted it. I must have been a bad girl. I do not for a split second believe now that what he did was my fault. I realized I was not a bad girl, and I did not do anything to warrant that kind of behavior. However, allowing it to happen was totally my fault. Even though I did not have the knowledge to defend myself. I had control over what happened to me.

Taking responsibility for others' actions has been a huge part of my life. Although my relationships have not been many, I have been cheated on several times. I always thought it was my fault, because I wasn't good enough, I wasn't pretty enough, I wasn't smart enough, or I wasn't enough for them. Every argument I ever encountered, I took responsibility for it being my fault.

When I was in a relationship, I would question unacceptable or shady behavior, then I would be made out to be the bad guy because I questioned. It was never their fault for doing wrong or acting inappropriately; it was my fault for questioning. Then I got accused of cheating because I was the one not trusting. I never liked confrontations and upsetting the apple cart, but I did want to know the truth. Maybe the relationship would be all peachy if I just kept my mouth shut and admitted I was wrong for questioning their actions. Maybe everybody would just be happy and not be mad or upset with me if I just did what they wanted me to do. I didn't like when people were mad at me, and to know I started the fight bothered me. I always wanted everyone to like me. Is that why I entered abusive relationship after abusive relationship? I am not sure, but I do know I looked for someone to like me, to love me, and ultimately to make me happy. I ran into dead-end relationships time after time. The type of guys I was attracted to were bad, egotistical, arrogant, down-right narcissistic guys.

I had to realize I was never going to be the same after the accident, not my body, my mind, or my attitude. I have experienced pain somewhere in my body every single day. I see that scar every day, multiple times a day, and it makes me sick to my stomach. I am grateful to be alive, but I am pissed off some days, too. My attitude still wavers back and forth from happy to sad. But now my mind was in a wonderful new place for once. I know I have made some bad decisions so far in my life, but it could have been a whole lot worse. I was not and never will be perfect, but I am much more aware of my thoughts, feelings, and decision-making choices. *No more choosing bad mates, blaming myself, and holding grudges.*

The Healing Begins

*"Knowing yourself is the beginning
of all wisdom."*

—ARISTOTLE

I WAS ON A ROAD TO RECOVERY. A long, hard, windy, curvy, uphill, downhill, emotional road, but one I was willing to travel. I knew it had to be done, physically, mentally, and emotionally. I made a commitment to go all out, do whatever I needed to do to get better and heal, inside and out. I was super excited and super scared. I was ready to discover the new me.

A friend, Cherie Robson, reached out to me during that time. I was fortunate to have met Cherie, as she was a major part of my recovery. Her husband and Matt worked together in the construction world. We met up with them on several occasions for dinner and boating and realized she and I had a ton in common. We became good friends, kept in touch, and traveled similar paths. I will hold her near and dear to my heart always! She is a Reiki practitioner and offered to do Reiki on me to help my healing. I had heard of this before but did not know what it was or how it worked exactly; however, I was willing to do, try, and have anything I could get my hands on. It's not that I was looking for a quick fix or expecting to be miraculously healed after one session, but I was looking for things to help me emotionally and physically outside of traditional medicine.

Because I could not drive, she offered to come to my house, which worked out well, as my boys were gone, and Matt was at the gym. We needed peace and quiet as well as privacy.

Cherie talked about energy and healing as she described this new and crazy procedure. She said, "Reiki is using energy to help the body heal itself. Sometimes health issues can be caused from blocked or stagnant energy in our energy centers, called chakras. Reiki helps unclog those blockages so the energy of the body can move freely and unobstructed. I will not be using my own energy to heal but calling on God or an ascended Master to assist with the process. I am just the conduit for the healing, not the healer. A person will not be healed if they do not want to be healed." I definitely wanted to be healed.

She told me she would hover her hands over certain parts of my body to read the energy radiating from that chakra. She would be starting with my root chakra, which is around the hip area.

She said it would be best to lie flat in a comfortable position. My mind said, *Halt right there,* and I had a quick wave of panic. I couldn't lie flat; it hurt my back and stomach too much. I had an incision down my entire belly and chest, a hole in my left side, ten broken ribs, and two fractured vertebrae! I couldn't get comfortable in any position but lying flat was not an option.

Using several pillows to prop me up, we managed to get me as reclined as we could on the chaise part of my couch—the piece of furniture I had been calling bed for the last few weeks. She put on some soft, meditation-type music and explained further what she was going to do. I had complete trust and faith in Cherie that everything was going to be OK. I had not known her very long and was not familiar with Reiki, but I had total belief; I knew she was special. She was taking time out of her busy, crazy, hectic schedule to come to my aid; that itself meant tons to me. She was willing to share with me a precious gift and talent she possessed. I greatly appreciated any time and help she was willing to offer, for she was a caregiver, a helper, a leader, and a mentor. There was a connection between us as we talked about healing mentally and physically. Cherie was soft spoken and caring and had a calm demeanor with a look of compassion in her eyes.

She moved slowly but with confidence as she demonstrated how Reiki worked. She always asked permission to touch my body before putting her hands on me. At first, I lay there with my eyes open, nervous or maybe anxious, but then slowly I was able to relax a little, and finally I closed my eyes. *Mission accomplished.* It was the most relaxed and comfortable I had been in a very, very long time. She started to use her "magic." She felt my chakra energy and tried to read what was going on with me then filled my body with positive things, probably more mentally and spiritually, but I was not sure. She taught me about chakras and energies and her ability to feel and read my energies to determine where I needed the most healing. It sounded fabulous to me.

When my session was over, I witnessed the most amazing feeling of relaxation, peace, and hope. My body felt energized and alive for the first time in weeks. I was so very grateful for my new guardian angel and overjoyed someone like her cared enough about me to share that knowledge with me. It was a spiritual feeling I had never experienced before but definitely hoped to experience again.

"WOW, that was awesome! I have never experienced anything like that!" I gratefully told her.

She shared with me areas of her concern and where she felt I needed the most healing: my throat, heart, and solar plexus chakras (the solar plexus is the stomach area). From what I understand, chakras can get blocked and not allow energy to flow through the body due to emotional upset or even accidents. The throat chakra, or fifth chakra, represents speaking and being able to express ourselves. It also represents creativity. The heart chakra is our fourth chakra and relates to love, joy, and decision-making abilities. The third chakra or solar plexus chakra is where our self-esteem and confidence stem from.

Cherie offered to come back again the next weekend, so we set up another appointment. All I could think was *Heck yeah, you can come anytime.*

After she left, I sat there feeling incredible. my first Reiki experience was amazing. Maybe she was able to unblock some of that bad, ol,' ugly, pent-up anger and pain I had been hoarding for quite some time. I rehashed what just happened, took in every feeling, every thought, every emotion, everything. I was not surprised I needed healing in my heart and stomach areas, but my throat was a little of a shock. I was grateful for Cherie—what a divine woman! She is a nurse, works long hours, takes care of her husband who has spinal stenosis, goes to school, is writing a book, and goes to the gym on a regular basis. This lady is amazing, truly amazing. She is definitely an angel. She is my angel. And she found time to help me. *I guess people really do care about me!*

Things were starting to look up for me. I had an amazing day after that Reiki session. I continued to have more energy mentally and physically than I had had in a long time. I had a way better attitude and felt more gratitude than ever. I had a strange warm kind of feeling throughout my body. *I like that Reiki stuff,* I said to myself. *Yep, Cherie is a divine messenger and was sent here to help me heal physically and spiritually.*

I was trying to grasp what was going on with my body, mind, and soul. I had not experienced that feeling before, so I just sat there quietly, savoring every moment. For once in my life I decided not to try to figure anything out. I tried to just be. That was so calming and peaceful and very different than how I usually operated.

With my Catholic upbringing I never felt or understood spirituality; I knew religion and "the Holy Spirit." Well, I knew of them, but I didn't really understand the Holy Spirit either. Maybe I was too young or was never interested, but I didn't remember much of my teachings on religion and still don't to this day.

To me, religion is some sort of organization where people with the same beliefs get together for worship or celebration of faith. Catholicism, Lutheranism, or Methodism are just some examples of religion to me. Spirituality is more of an individual belief in someone or something greater than ourselves that we turn to for answers and guidance. It is not an organization or gathering. It may or may not necessarily be God, but it is divine and immaterial. I do believe in God, and I do believe there is something greater than ourselves. I am spiritual but do not practice or belong to an organized religion. I do believe in prayer and doing the right thing. I do believe in signs from God or our spiritual world—I do wish these were a little more obvious sometimes, like maybe a text message or an email. I don't really comprehend it all, but I continue to learn and broaden my knowledge through reading and discussions with Lynn. She helps me tremendously with Scripture from the Bible and with how to be a good person. I love her with all my heart.

I kept in close contact with Cherie over the next few days regarding my healing. She was very knowledgeable, caring, and super compassionate. I'll bet she is an amazing nurse, for she really cares for people and about people. She knew a lot about angels, chakra energy, and the body-mind connection. I felt like I could talk with her for hours.

Cherie was the one who told me about the book, *You Can Heal Your Life*, by Louise Hay. I love to read, so this was a book I knew I had to have. She told me about meditation and all sorts of things I was not familiar with: Reiki, energy, angels, and meditation. I wanted to know it all. I wanted everything to help me heal—mentally, physically, spiritually. I needed to get in touch with myself.

I was so excited for my new healing journey. I finally had a direction. I always liked knowing where I was going and liked having a plan. I knew in my head this was going to be a process, but I was excited to learn new things and help my body and mind heal. I was getting some positivity back into my life, and I knew that was going to be profound. I have never experienced injuries to this extent, so I did not know how to heal mentally, spiritually, or even physically. I always thought the physical part of healing just happened — *time heals all wounds, right?* But I realized I needed some serious help in healing physically as well. I liked the Eastern medicine side to healing so all this was what I craved.

I have another amazing friend, Dr. Carrie Wolf. She is a fabulous chiropractor in Parker, Colorado, and was also a huge component to my healing. I had met her through my network marketing company several years before. She had heard of my accident and reached out to see how she could help. Carrie is truly awesome; she also came to my house in snowstorms to help me. *How cool is that?* She brought PEMF (pulsed electromagnetic field) mats, large and small, and showed me how to use them. She explained these mats deliver electromagnetic pulses to the body, improving circulation to areas to promote healing and overall wellness. Lying on them a couple of times a day would be beneficial to promote my healing.

She taped my back and ribs with Rock Tape to help relieve some pressure and help with inflammation. Rock Tape is considered a therapeutic, topical pain relief, kinesiology tape that helps alleviate inflammation and provides support for joints. She also adjusted my neck and back while I was standing upright and eventually rubbed my shoulders. I didn't realize how sore and stiff my body was getting from sitting around until she rubbed my shoulders. And most important, she hugged me. That was probably one of the best treatments ever. People were reluctant to hug me for fear they would hurt me, but she was gentle. Hugs were just what I needed and craved, but nobody seemed to be giving them out. She also brought me amazing socks that were fluffy and lined with aloe. Those things were awesome. After all, it was February in Colorado, and we were in for record snowfall and cold temperatures.

I was talking with Carrie on the phone as she was on her way over the first time. "I just pulled into your cul-de-sac," she said. "I'll be right in." I informed her my door was unlocked and to just come in. I waited and waited and waited. *Surely, she should be to my door by now.* I got up to go look out the front door. It was icy and snowing, so I didn't dare go outside to look, but I was worried for my friend. All of a sudden, she came around the corner with a huge grin on her face. She had gone to the neighbor's house. Keep in mind she was supposed to just come right in, so she just walked right into my neighbor's house. I guess they were both shocked. This might not be as funny to you as it was to me, but my sister and another friend had done the exact same thing a few days earlier. I bet my neighbors started locking their door.

Carrie was a big reader and had some recommendations for me on books to read, CDs to listen to, and

YouTube videos to watch. After she left, I thought she, too, was an angel sent to help me heal. My Divine Team was awesome, and I was seeing it in action.

Positivity was an important factor in my adult life; it wasn't always easy to sustain, but it was something I always pondered. I don't remember as a child knowing anything about positive thoughts or practicing such behavior. Most of my life involved staying in survival mode, not participating in positive thought-provoking activities. I was good at negativity and how to think negative, wicked thoughts about myself. I knew bad things happened more than positive ones.

Somewhere along my network marketing path I developed the belief that if you think positively, positive things would happen. I never lived by that concept when I was younger or experienced much success. I would say the words but didn't feel the feeling or put it into practice. For once in my life, I was feeling the effects of living by the positive words I was saying and thinking. I do believe if you put feeling into those thoughts, they will happen. You get what you think about. I was concentrating on specific healing about my physical status, and I was getting better, I was getting stronger, and I was feeling more energy. I was reading material based on constructive, productive outcomes and goals that were attainable. I could see a change in my attitude. I wanted to be better, do better for everyone in my life, including myself. I wanted to be the best mom, wife, sister, daughter, and friend anyone could ask for. I wanted to be a mentor to others. I wanted to help. I wanted to feel alive and worthy.

Loving Me

"Thoughts become things, make them good ones."

—MIKE DOOLEY

I SPENT A LOT OF TIME ON MY IPAD watching videos, listening to powerful and successful people like Louise Hay, Bob Proctor, Deepak Chopra, Wayne Dyer, Jim Rohn, and Zig Ziglar. With a team like that and my Divine Team behind me, I knew I was going to succeed. I knew I was going to make it. And I knew I was going to be better than before. It was up to me now.

I started reading *You Can Heal Your Life*. When I read a book, I usually underline or highlight things that pertain to me, then I go back and read the book again focusing on the highlighted portions. The first few chapters of Louise Hay's book, I highlighted everything, every word, every sentence. I made notes in the margins. I was so intrigued by this book that I didn't want to put it down. I could totally connect to what this woman was writing; she was amazing to me.

I learned things like my thoughts created my life, my situations, and my results. I learned that if I was focused on being sick, I would be sick. If I focused on being disease free, I would get better. This was huge for me because I lay there day after day, week after week, being told by my doctors that I had fluid around my lung, and I might need surgery. My liver was badly bruised, my ribs would always hurt, I had polyps on my vocal cords, and would need surgery. They found two more broken ribs on the right side in the front. My blood work was still out of whack. I had no spleen, so I was going to be sick all the time because my immune system was compromised. I was probably going to get pneumonia and end up back in the hospital. No wonder I was a wreck, physically and mentally. My doctors were focused on the dis-ease in my body, not on how to make me better. I believed everything the doctors were telling me. and it usually wasn't good news. I was focused on what was wrong with me instead of how to heal. Up to that point, I researched all the sickness parts of what was going on instead of the how-to-heal-and-get-better parts. Once I learned that your life and results go where your focus is, I felt I was always going to be sick, so I knew I had to shift my thinking, and shift it quickly.

I started reading and researching about the Law of Attraction. I used to believe on a small level that you get what you think about; you attract things to you, good or bad. So, I had decided in my mind to start focusing on good thoughts, positive thoughts to aid in my healing and my overall wellbeing. I realized through the learning process that this Law of Attraction was much bigger and more powerful than I ever imagined. This was something I needed to study, learn, and apply to my life.

Thanks to Louise Hay and the Law of Attraction, I said, "No more being sick." I was not having another surgery, I was going to be fine, and I was going to start healing my body and most important, my mind. I was seriously tired of being sick and tired. I had heard that expression before, but I was honestly living it. I wanted healing and peace in my body and my mind. I took every word Louise spoke to me to heart. She was an integral part of my healing and changing my thinking around. I will be forever grateful for her.

I started listening to Louise on YouTube. I needed to know everything she had to say. I felt like my higher power was speaking to me through her. I know some of you might think that sounds weird, but I believe divine intervention was happening right then and there. My answers were coming to me loud and clear. My prayers were being answered. I probably had had many prayers answered in the past and missed them because I wasn't listening well enough. Now I was quiet enough to listen, I was READY to listen, and I heard it loud and clear. I was ready to receive what she was teaching me. I have never experienced this before and knew I needed it more than ever.

What I was hearing most was that I need to love myself. *What? Love myself?* I was raised to take care of everyone else first; loving yourself was egotistical, selfish, and wrong. It seemed a little weird to me, loving myself. I never knew how to love myself, not even respect myself; heck, I didn't even know myself. I wondered if this was going to be a hard one for me, but I knew how much of an impact this would make on my new life, so I was willing to give it my all. Louise Hay wanted me to stand in front of the mirror and talk to myself, tell myself, "I love you and respect you." My first thought was there was no way, no way I was doing that. Then I reminded myself if I wanted to get better this was what I must do. I had to get out of my comfort zone. If I wanted different results with my life, I had to do something different. I trusted Louise and knew she would not lead me astray.

I worked with a life coach about four years ago who introduced me to mirror work, so this was not the first time I had to look at myself in the mirror. *Mirror, mirror on the wall, who is the fairest of them all? Was it me?* I was supposed to think it was me, but I didn't. My previous mirror work involved me looking at myself for one solid minute without saying anything. That, too, was hard at first, but I did master it, so I knew I would be able to do this work suggested by Louise. This was the first time I had to tell myself, "I love you."

I stood in front of that mirror and saw a worn-down, beat-up old lady who was broken inside and out. *How on earth am I going to tell her I love her? Whew ... this is going to be hard.* I started slowly, just making eye contact for fifteen seconds then eventually graduating to a full minute of eye contact. I felt awkward and strange staring at myself in the mirror. My personality forced me to keep going until I successfully said the words out loud, "I love you," while maintaining eye contact. Wow! That was uncomfortable. I felt embarrassed. Then the tears slowly started to roll down my face until I was crying hard with no breaks between the tears. But I continued to make eye contact and repeat, "I love you," "I love you, Diane." I remained still, looking myself in the eyes with no words, for what seemed like hours. Finally, I felt relief and reassurance; I knew I did love myself, I did care, I did matter, and I was important. Mirror work might seem silly at first, but it is very gratifying.

I was going to have to work on loving my body again. I wasn't too pleased with it. I had a 12-inch scar from the middle of my chest way down past and around my belly button to my pubic bone. The surgeon didn't even make the scar straight; it is crooked as it goes around my belly button. I thought it looked hideous. I realized deep down that scar saved my life, so I knew it had to be there. However, I didn't have to like it; in fact, I hated it. I didn't have the best body in the world, but as a fitness competitor, I can say I had an eight-pack at one point. Now I had a scar and a very ugly scar at that. I hated my body and I resented that scar.

That was a huge setback for me. I was having a very hard time dealing with that blemish. I kept reminding myself that I should be grateful to be alive, and that scar was there to save my life. It was hard to do, but I persevered and continued to work on loving that scar. Friends and family called it my beauty mark, my bravery mark, my battle scar, my new birthmark for my new life. On the surface I could accept this, but not deep down. I just couldn't. I was very bitter. I was afraid people, especially Matt, were going to be repulsed by it. Surely, he had to be; I certainly was.

I am sure some of you think that is absolutely absurd to be bothered by a scar, but I was. Part of me was ashamed for my negative thinking because it was "just a scar." There are so many people out there with far more issues than a scar down the middle of their belly. But I thought it was ugly and made my stomach look odd. I dwelled on the ugliness. I knew I had to stop the crazy swirling thoughts and preach to myself. I was the one who ultimately had to make peace with it, not Matt or anyone else. It was my scar and I had to own it. Not yet though—I was not ready to accept it. I realized this was going to require some work, which I was willing to do. I knew I needed to get past this issue.

Over the next few weeks I continued watching Louise Hay's *10 Steps to Loving Yourself* and *The Universe Loves Grateful People* on YouTube. I had read her book and highlighted almost every word. I felt like I was feeling better. I felt like I was making progress, mentally, spiritually, and physically. I was feeling amazing compared to where I came from, but I was still missing something. I still wasn't as content as I wanted to be. I wasn't where I wanted to be with loving myself yet, and I knew it was going to take time. I was not about to quit or give up. I just kept moving forward with dedication and patience.

It finally happened right there in my living room! It wasn't a single event that triggered the desire to change. After several grueling weeks, months, and years of feeling deflated and disappointed, my frustration escalated to the breaking point. I was tired of waiting for others to make me happy. I decided I was worth it, I was important, and I deserved my own love and attention. I needed to treat me like someone I loved and cared about. I decided to go within and get what I wanted, to treat myself like I wanted to be treated. I was going to love myself the way I wanted to be loved. But most important, I was going to nurture myself for the first time in my life. I was going to be there for me! I had these expectations of how I wanted to be treated and cared for, and these expectations were not getting met. *So, who better to care for those needs than me?* Not that anyone was doing anything wrong by any means. It was just that I needed love and nurturing from myself. I needed to make myself feel special and important. I was the only one from whom I needed acceptance.

As I moved along in my personal growth and development journey, I remember reading and hearing about the importance of always looking within when there are problems. I had actually never grasped that concept before. You know how you read things but never carry out the lesson? Lord knows, I have done that plenty of times. I think of Jim Rohn when he tells the story of how he wrote down all these excuses and reasons why he had not been successful, then he threw that list away and wrote the word "me" at the top of his next list. He realized the only reason he had not reached his goals of success was because of himself, no outside source or circumstance. I wrote "me" on the top of my paper that day. I needed to love ME!

It was that realization that brought me to the reason for the accident. It was to teach me how to love and respect myself. It was to teach me to look within. It was to teach me how to be the amazing person that I was put here to be and to go help others who struggled with low self-esteem, no self- love, or lack of confidence. Finally, it came to me. I knew the reason. I knew my purpose for my life! And I was so grateful for the chance to share with others. *Wow, what a responsibility! My Higher Power has a plan for me, and now I know what that plan is.* I liked to help people, so this was going to be very rewarding.

My purpose was to teach others the amazing lessons I learned. By loving and respecting yourself you can build self-esteem and stand up for yourself, build a better business, have better relationships, and be a better person. Imagine how this would change the world, if we could change one person at a time. Bring back the good we were put here for. It was spoken to me so clearly — go pursue your life-coaching career, go teach others what you know, go teach others the importance of loving thyself. Oh my, I felt like a ton of bricks were lifted. That day was the beginning of a new life for me. I was on a mission to go *save the world!* (One person at a time, of course.)

I wanted to start with kids, my kids. I wanted to teach them how to love themselves and build good strong relationships. I wanted to explain to my boys how to think good positive thoughts and be confident. I wanted to share ideas with a husband who loved me the way I would love myself to strengthen our relationship. I wanted to teach kids how to love and respect themselves so they would not be abused, sexually, physically, or mentally. I wanted to teach everyone all about the Law of Attraction. You get what you think about; make the thoughts good ones!

My Voice

"If you get tired, learn to rest, not to quit."

—L'HISTOIRE DERRIÈRE BANKSY

MY VOCAL CORDS HAD TAKEN A BEATING, and developed polyps with two surgeries and intubations under my belt. Even though the surgeries were seven months apart, my voice at times was hoarse, while other times it would fade in and out, change octaves, or go completely silent. It had a mind of its own. I sounded like a three-pack-a-day smoker at times or a teenager going through puberty. You know the high voice and the low voice all within the same word? People could not understand me or hear me, and I was getting super frustrated.

I would go to the store and people would treat me as if I were hearing impaired and mentally impaired. They would talk to me slowly and loudly using hand gestures. It was like when we talk to people with a language barrier: we talk loudly and slowly, like that is going to help them understand a foreign language. I tried explaining my hearing and brain were fine, that it was just my voice that was messed up. When I realized my intelligence was being insulted, I was bothered by that. Big time.

During my meditation and journaling I discovered it upset me if people insinuated I wasn't smart. I know that I am not the smartest person, but I do consider myself to be pretty intelligent. But my intellect was being insulted. *Why is this so upsetting to me? Why do I care what other people think of my intelligence?*

Being smart meant I would be loved, I would be important, and I would be special: those old thoughts haunted me. And those childhood nightmares of need-ing to be smart were still haunting me, too. So, it was important to me to be smart, and I felt proud when I got to prove my knowledge. But I wanted to feel important to Matt, I wanted his love, and I wanted him to think I was special. I wanted so much for him to think I was smart. *How do I get him to make me feel special? How do I get him to make me feel important? How do I prove to him I am not stupid?* I finally realized I had to stop the downward spirals and remind myself I don't get HIM to make me feel any particular way; I get ME to make ME feel a certain way. I don't rely on Matt or anybody's mood, love, attention, or opinion to determine my feelings for myself.

After numerous visits to various ENT (ear, nose, and throat) specialists and laryngologists, they determined the polyps on my vocal cords were still present and told me I needed surgery to remove them. As an alternative to surgery, we could try treating them with steroids and ibuprofen, but success at removing them was unlikely. Plus, it would require that I ingest 800 mgs of ibuprofen four times a day.

"Oh yeah," the ENT said, "and you're also going to need Prilosec with all that ibuprofen, so you don't develop ulcers. We could also refer you to a voice specialist who can help you with your voice until surgery."

Wait! Another surgery? Or 800mgs of Ibuprofen four times a day? And they were going to have to intubate me, which was what caused this in the first place? Oh, hell no, I am not having that done. That made no sense to me, the medication regimen or the surgery. *No disrespect to my doctors, but I'm going to self-treat. I AM NOT HAVING ANOTHER SURGERY.* I decided to take matters into my own hands again with my body and healing. I was adamant about not having another tube down my throat.

I take an all-natural supplement that reduces inflammation I was introduced to through my network marketing company. I decided to take one capsule of my supplement every six hours instead of the ibuprofen; that way I wouldn't be burning my stomach or esophagus. As a distributor I cannot make any claims that the supplement treats, mitigates, or cures any diseases, but I do know what it has done for me and how it has helped my body.

After much deliberation I went to see the voice specialist to learn how to talk without stressing out my vocal cords. I did not think that was the answer to my problem, but I knew it couldn't hurt. I asked her if I would be able to sing after these lessons. She asked me if I could sing before my vocal cords were damaged.

"Of course not," I said. "That's why I am wondering."

She laughed as we continued with our lesson. It was very interesting therapy for me, like nothing I had ever experienced. She had me saying and using weird vowel sounds, like long eeeeeeeeee, drug-out short aaaaaaaaah, and long ooooooooooo. They seemed so funny they were hard to do without laughing. I think I was more embarrassed than anything. I had to do breathing exercises that required me to use my stomach instead of my lungs, which was new to me. I practiced what she taught me while in the car from time to time and resorted to what she taught me when I got stressed out or upset and my voice went out. Evidently, relaxing my vocal cords got my polyps under control so my voice worked.

My voice therapist also recommended slippery elm lozenges to assist in my voice recovery. There was a young girl at the health food store I reached out to while shopping for the lozenges. I mentioned I like the Eastern medicine healing philosophy, so I wanted natural things; I wanted holistic. She told me about dry brushing, where you take a soft brush of some sort and rub it over the throat before getting in the shower to increase circulation to that area. She told me that once the warm water hits the area that was dry-brushed, it might help reduce inflammation and the polyps by getting more circulation to the area. It sounded a little hocus-pocus to me, but I was willing to do anything. She instructed me not to get too aggressive with it, to just gently scratch my throat a little. Hocus-pocus, witchcraft, or just plain weird, I definitely was going to try.

I also reverted to what my friend Cherie told me about chakras and my throat chakra. I had no idea what that meant, but it sounded pretty interesting and important to my healing, so I started my new research project … the throat chakra!

What I learned was the throat chakra is the fifth of the seven chakras, or spiritual centers of the body. It obviously was located in the throat area and is said to represent creativity and expression. The throat is where change takes place, whether it is encouraging change or not allowing change, according to Louise Hay. *Hmmm, what exactly does that mean?* I had just been through a major change in my life physically, mentally, and emotionally. Normally, I'm a little hesitant with change; however, I didn't instigate this change or have any control over it, but I did have to deal with it. I have considered myself to be both creative and expressive, so how did that apply to my throat issue, or did it? I had to look into this further.

I researched more of what Louise Hay said about the throat. She says that the throat area "represents our ability to 'speak up' for ourselves." When we have throat problems, "we feel inadequate to stand up for ourselves." *Wow. That is pretty powerful.* Not being able to speak up for myself was definitely happening. Whenever I tried to express my concerns about the accident, whether it was the crash itself or what I was going through, I would shut myself down. I was afraid talking about it constantly would come across as being weak, insecure, and feeling sorry for myself.

I was not feeling sorry for myself now, but I badly needed to talk about this accident. I needed to rehash it, needed to ask what happened, needed to talk it through, and needed to put some closure to it. I found every time I started talking about it, especially with Matt, he didn't seem interested in hearing what I had to say. I respected the fact it was probably hard for him, too. He did not want to rehash any of it or hear about it anymore, so I clammed up. I needed to scream at the top of my lungs. I needed to express my feelings to move on and heal. I continued to say nothing and just worked on myself. I kept telling myself to be patient, that it would come. I knew keeping these thoughts locked up was not going to be good for me, so I needed to learn how to release these thoughts and feelings to myself.

Over time, through meditation and releasing anger, I was able to resolve most of my issues, at least with my throat. I know this might sound like totally strange, woohoo hippie, hard-to-believe voodoo stuff, but I swear after releasing my anger out loud about not being heard, the very next day my voice was fine and back to almost normal. I cancelled all my future appointments and never went back to the ENT, laryngologist, or voice therapy specialist. To this day I have not had any major problems with my vocal cords locking up on me or totally losing my voice. Granted, my voice is altered and deeper than before, but that is the new me, that is my new normal. I am not going to lie: some days I am bothered by my voice, but I just remind myself to be grateful that I have it.

Keep On Keepin' On

*"Never be ashamed of a scar. It simply means you were
stronger than whatever tried to hurt you."*

—ANONYMOUS

I CONTINUED WORKING ON LOVING my body and all
my imperfections. That was very hard for me, maybe
because I was a visual person, and I realized my body
was never going to look the same ever again. It was
changed forever. I was trying to appreciate all that it
had been through, but I still was holding a lot of anger. I
was not quite sure who or what I was angry with. I just
knew I was angry. *Who am I kidding? I am downright pissed
off. Am I pissed at the surgeon who cut my belly crooked?
Couldn't he at least have cut it straight? Instead of cutting
down the middle and around my belly button, maybe he could*

have cut a straight line off to the side. Would *that have made me happy?* That incision was permanent; it was NEVER going away. I knew this was a wrong attitude about it, so I decided to forgive the surgeon for not cutting me open the way I wanted him to and tried to move on.

I learned this forgiveness technique from Louise Hay: forgive someone or something for not being the way you want them to be, then let it go. I also made a mental note to myself that this area needed more of my attention. I needed to learn to accept my scar, learn to love my body the way it was, learn to love my new look. This was not going to be easy, but it *was* necessary.

My friend Carrie knew how bothered I was by that scar, so she loaned me a Chattanooga Ultrasound machine. It heats muscle tissue to help break up scarring and promote healing. I used that thing every day, twice a day, while forgiving the surgeon for not cutting me straight.

Through meditation and listening to Louise Hay I kept hearing, "Love your body right where it is at." I decided to put myself mentally in the same boat as someone who wanted to lose weight. *What would I tell them?* I would tell them to love their body where it is while working on getting the weight off. It takes time and patience. I needed to practice what I preached. I needed to love, respect, and appreciate my body, right here, right now. Time would heal a lot if I could just be patient. Patience was something I was never good at, but I am not a quitter. I knew I would conquer this.

I recognized and appreciated that my body had been through an enormous amount of trauma. I also realized that I was truly grateful I was alive, and I was grateful I wasn't hurt more than I was. What an eye opener that statement was for me—*Be grateful I wasn't hurt more.* I knew my situation could have been so much worse for me and for Matt. One of us could have died, we could have been paralyzed, or we could have brain damage. Even though I realized all of this, recovery was still difficult. With a lot of meditation, I determined my body was amazing; it had protected me. It literally had protected me from getting completely crushed. My doctors kept telling me how lucky it was I was in great shape, in good health, and had a strong core. My rib cage was strong and an awesome protector, my skin held everything together, and my heart was strong and healthy. I finally started to focus on all the things my body had done for me, instead of the scars it had suffered from protecting me. I realized I was blessed, truly blessed.

To this day, deep down, I am still saddened and sickened by that scar, but I continue to work on acceptance. I know it is easier for me to respect my body because it did protect me, but loving it 100%? I still need to work on that. I thought about getting my scar tattooed to look like a zipper or flower vines. Although I have not pulled the trigger on that one yet, I ponder the thought from time to time.

During my healing journey, I stumbled across a video on YouTube called *Breaking the Terror Barrier* by Bob Proctor. *Holy cow, what an amazing eye opener for me!* The video is about our conscious and subconscious minds, how our thoughts got there, how they related to our emotions, and what to do about the thoughts. This made so much sense to me. Years of traditional therapy taught me about my feelings and how certain things made me feel. Feel, feel, feel. But not once did I learn where those feelings came from, how they got there, or how those feelings were connected to my thoughts, and I certainly didn't know how to get rid of or change them.

I assumed because I had a screwed-up past, I was supposed to have sad, negative, and bitter feelings. From Bob Proctor's video I learned about reprogramming my subconscious mind to get rid of bad, ugly thoughts so my feelings would change, too. Another miracle was put before me.

I had been aware of my bad, negative feelings for years but didn't know how to deal with them. It drove me crazy because I wanted these feelings to go away. I wanted to feel differently about myself but did not know how. I used to think that maybe if I forgave people, maybe if I tried harder to be a better person, I wouldn't have so many negative self-loathing feelings. Although I had read books and sought therapy, I had nothing in my tool box on how to get rid of my pessimistic feelings.

After I watched the *Terror Barrier* video, I learned that my feelings came from thoughts, which have created my paradigms. We have all heard of paradigm shifts, but I didn't know how to shift anything, especially my mind or thoughts. Were all these negative thoughts in my subconscious mind making me have screwed up feelings? Oh my gosh, that was another aha moment for me. Remember, I am a big "why" person. If I know why, I can cope much better. After all these years, I finally knew why I had no self-esteem or confidence! It was like a ton of bricks had been lifted off my back and potentially out of my mind. I was responsible for those thoughts. I was fueling my bad, screwed up, negative feelings because of my bad, screwed up, negative thoughts. I was in total control of my own thoughts, regardless of how they got there.

I was responsible for my bad thoughts twirling around in my mind. *Hmm, interesting, so how do I get them out of my head? How do I get rid of them? How do I release bad thoughts?*

In Proctor's video he talked about releasing techniques to rid your mind of the negative thoughts. I practiced these release techniques to start weeding out bad thoughts once and for all.

It was pretty amazing to me, because I am a "go to the source" kind of person. *Was this a straight shot to the source or what?* I learned my subconscious mind was my source of all the negative thoughts, and I was relieved to know there was help for me. When I was in traditional therapy, counselors talked about peeling back the layers of the onion. I wanted to slice that sucker in half, because I'm not patient enough to go one layer at a time to resolve my issues. *Let's get right to the middle, get right to the source.* For me, going straight to the thoughts was going right to the heart of the source. If I could change my thoughts, I would change my life. *How powerful!*

Bob Proctor talked about his experience with Napoleon Hill's book, *Think and Grow Rich.* That book evidently changed Bob's life and way of thinking, so, of course, I figured that was a book I needed since I wanted to change my life. I had heard of *Think and Grow Rich* before but never read it. After reading it, I strongly suggest you read *Think and Grow Rich.*

I combined what I learned from Louise Hay and Rhonda Byrne about the Law of Attraction with what I had learned from Bob Proctor and Napoleon Hill to put together a much clearer picture of what was going on in my head. For the first time in fifty years I finally felt like I understood something about myself, my mind, my soul, and my being. I had to work with my thoughts more, not so much my feelings, and what I put out into the universe, I would get back. What an amazing discovery that was for me, and I was super excited to learn more and see the results.

As I reflected on my past, I realized I attracted the good as well as the bad. From now on, I was going to try my best to focus only on good, happy, and positive things.

Letting Go of the Past

"Be the change you wish to see in the world."

—GANDHI

BEING AWARE THAT WHAT I PUT OUT in the universe was based on my thoughts prompted me to learn more, study more, research more. *How do I literally change my thoughts after fifty years of thinking a certain way?* I was not quite sure how, but I was more than willing to find out.

Bob Proctor taught me that you don't necessarily have to know how you are going to get where you want to be. You just need to know what you want, and the things you need will come before you. I definitely knew what I wanted. I wrote it out, read it over several times, and engrained in my mind what I wanted. I wanted to know and fully understand what my thoughts were, where they were coming from, and how they got in my head.

I knew I wanted to be happy and appreciate things. I wanted to feel grateful for all the wonderful things and people I had in my life. I wanted to be successful in my business relationships and life. I wanted to feel important to my boys, my family, and Matt. I wanted to know and feel that I mattered to others as well as myself. I wanted to feel better physically, mentally, and emotionally. I wanted to think positively. I wanted a better life. I wanted a better me. For once in my life I wanted self-esteem and confidence. I wanted to be an inspiration to others.

While at Barnes & Noble to purchase *Think and Grow Rich*, I came across *You Are the Placebo*, by Dr. Joe Dispenza, a book about the mind and body connection on a cellular level. I wasn't looking for this book, but I feel like it found me. As a science person I wanted to study what was going on in my mind and body during recovery, and the book sounded intriguing. I certainly needed to read it. I purchased both books.

Dr. Dispenza talked about things such as epigenetics and healing your body through thoughts. I also discovered I cannot have a new future if I am still living in the past. That hit home hard and was TOTALLY what I needed. I have always lived in the past and have not been willing to let go for some reason. I wanted a different outcome and a better future. I yearned for a different life, but my negative thought process kept me locked in the past. No wonder I wasn't going where I wanted with my personal life or in business. My old thoughts and paradigms had not changed. I needed to change my way of thinking and rewire my brain to think differently if I wanted different results. It occurred to me that for years I had dedicated time to care for the outside of my body, but never my mind. My mind now needed a workout; it was time for a mind boot camp.

Dr. Dispenza says epigenetics is the "control of genes not from within the DNA itself but from messages coming from outside the cell." My definition of epigenetics is conditioning the brain to a new thought process, so it sends new signals for a different result. So, if I kept thinking the same thoughts and holding the same beliefs about my life, my brain would continue sending the same messages to the same genes, and I would keep going down the road with no change.

According to Dr. Dispenza, "Only when the cell is ignited in a new way, by new information, can it create thousands of variations of the same gene to rewrite a new expression of proteins which change the body." Learning a new thing was going to literally change my brain cells and alter my genes, so I could potentially be successful in change. I could rewire my brain and reprogram it to think differently than it ever had before.

Even though I considered myself to be a fairly positive person, I had a horrible habit of thinking negatively, mostly about myself. For example, when someone didn't want to join my network marketing business, my old thought process started the downward spiral that I was not good enough, I was not smart enough, or there must be something wrong with me. My new thought process would stop this negative thinking in its tracks. I would focus on positive and real aspects of the situation, such as telling myself the person was simply not interested in my product or business and their participation was no reflection on me or my intelligence. I had to learn not to take rejection personally; it had nothing to do with me or my past. Wow! That was going to be a hard one for me, because I seemed to take everything personally.

My old thought process of being cheated on was along the same lines, that I must not be good enough, not be smart enough, and must certainly not be pretty enough. However, my new thought process needed to stop the negativity and understand the reality. I wasn't being cheated on because I wasn't good enough, smart enough, or pretty enough. He cheated because there was a problem with him; he had the issue! I wasn't saying I did not have issues that I brought to a relationship, but his cheating was not my fault. His cheating was because he was a loser and not content with himself. Again, he had nothing to do with me, but I took it personally. Not anymore.

Most important, my new thought process needed to focus on positive attributes, positive thoughts, and positive outcomes regardless of the situation. No more negative thinking about myself or my past. No more taking things personally.

I needed to change myself in order to be able to help others with their changes. As Gandhi said, "Be the change you wish to see in the world." I needed to be the change I wanted to see in me. I could not rely on anyone else anymore to make me feel a certain way; it was up to me.

Discovering Success

"Almost every successful person begins with two beliefs: the future can be better than the present, and I have the power to make it so."

—DAVID BROOKS

I WANTED WHAT SUCCESSFUL PEOPLE HAD, but what was it they had? I started my adventure to find out. I immediately thought of people I know in my network marketing business, so I made my list of who I wanted to study. I decided to research successful people. Why are they doing well? Why are their businesses growing while others stay the same? What are they doing right and what are they doing wrong?

My first thought was to reach out to one of the most amazing women I have ever met, Carrie Dickie. She was one of the top distributors in my network marketing company. I met her at business events in California. I liked her— no, loved her—instantly. To say she's awesome is an understatement. She is kind, considerate, and carefree. Carrie is happy living in the moment and loving life. She taught me to love everything and everyone. Go out into the world and have fun, she would say, and love everybody. I was truly inspired by this woman and wanted to have more love in my heart for everyone like she did. I have learned a lot from her and know I will continue to learn more from this amazing woman. She is a great example of success, not only in her business, but also in life. I am very grateful to call her my friend.

Another amazing mentor of mine is Greg Dieker. I also met him through my network marketing business in Denver. He is part of my "upline" and one of the top income earners in the company, so I reached out to him to learn about success. I felt like he took me under his wing to show me the ropes on building a network of people. He was a straight shooter, so instantly I had a lot of respect for this man, as I like straight to the point. He's strong, assertive, confident, and very supportive, personally and in my business. Greg taught me to believe in myself, have confidence, and just share the products and business opportunity with people. He has great morals and values, which are two things I appreciate. I have always looked up to him and will be forever grateful for getting to meet him. He is a dear business partner and friend.

After interviewing other successful people I knew who owned their own business outside of my company, I came to this conclusion: all successful people seem to be at peace. I always thought they were at peace because of money. Certainly, money helps, but I discovered they all had a few other things in common. First, they all had a spiritual belief, some higher power they worshiped. I felt they also all loved and respected themselves. *That's it; that's the key: love and respect myself. If I get right with myself by learning how to love, respect, and appreciate yours truly, I can be successful in business, relationships, and my life!* I started to see a common theme here. Do you see it as well? Do you see how loving and respecting ourselves can have a major impact on our lives?

It is like the analogy of putting my oxygen mask on first before I can help others. Are you familiar with that flight attendant's safety speech? They say to put on your own oxygen mask first so you will be able to assist others. If you don't get your mask on and get the oxygen you need, you will be of no service to anyone else.

After I finished my Louise Hay book, I started reading *Think and Grow Rich.* They say if you want to be successful, you have to think like successful people, and you have to hang out with successful people. I had eight books to read and I wanted to read them all at once. I wanted to know everything right away. I felt I couldn't get the knowledge fast enough. It had been only three weeks since the accident and I was grateful I was not back to work yet, as I had a lot of learning and studying to do. I did not have time for work.

What an amazing book, *Think and Grow Rich*. All this time I thought the book was about acquiring riches; however, there was a lot more valuable information in there. Hill talks about thoughts and goals. Thinking about what you want will come to you, so make sure your thoughts are positive. You can acquire money by thinking like rich people. And goals—having goals, writing goals, achieving goals—were all important to success. It was certainly life changing for me and my thought process. Again, if you have not read that book, I would highly suggest you read it.

Hill made me realize several things about thoughts and goals, but what impacted me the most was the fact that "we have absolute control over our own thoughts." That was pretty powerful and profound to me. It dawned on me nobody has made me think one way or the other; I have done that all on my own. I was in total control over all my thoughts all those years. Granted, people planted ideas in my head both intentionally and inadvertently, but it was what I chose to do with those thoughts that really mattered. So far in my life I had not done a very good job with my thoughts. I let them control me; I never controlled them.

Think and Grow Rich was written in 1937, so that thought process has been around for years. *Where had I been?* I wished I had read that book years ago, and I wished its lessons were taught in school. Controlling your own thoughts, having goals, and thinking positively are concepts I would love to teach to younger people, especially my own kids.

Journaling

"If you don't make peace with your past, it will keep showing up in your present."

—WAYNE DYER

SITTING AROUND DAY AFTER DAY thinking and thinking, I realized a lot of things. I realized I was frustrated in my business, my career, and my relationships. I was frustrated with my life. I didn't even know specifically what I wanted anymore because I had lost focus over the years. I was always a go-getter, an ambitious person, and I felt I had lost all of that. I wanted to know why. *What happened to me?* I finally was at a place mentally with my recovery where I could use the time off wisely to learn characteristics about myself and how to get my life back on track. It had been four weeks since the accident, and I was not seeing work in my future anytime soon.

I needed to learn how to love and respect myself. I needed to learn how to be more successful in business and in my relationships; I needed my life back. I wanted success; I wanted happiness.

I started journaling more and more. Journaling always seemed time consuming and frustrating to me. My thoughts were always so much faster than my hand. I wanted to write as fast as I could think, but it was impossible. One thing I had learned since the accident was I could not move as fast as I used to physically or mentally. I used to eat fast, drive fast, talk fast, walk fast — everything was fast. Maybe this was a sign to slow down in every aspect of my life. Physically I had to slow down; I literally could not move nearly as fast as normal for me. With all my injuries I had to move with care and caution. Mentally I needed to slow down as well, which I noticed big time with my journaling. I needed to relax, take a deep breath, and gather my thoughts. I needed to take one thing at a time that I wanted to work on or learn, then journal about it, whether it was a negative thought or just one word.

I would grab my notebook and favorite mechanical pencil. (I love using mechanical pencils.) I coached myself to take my time to think about what I wanted to write then write. There was no reason to hurry, I was not going anywhere, and there was nowhere I had to be. I wrote about areas in my life I wanted to pay attention to: business, personal relationships, me, career, life. I needed to pay attention to my life. I needed to pay attention to ME!

I started with my network marketing business. I had not been involved wholeheartedly in months. I did not quit, but I did not have the burning desire I had when I first started. I asked myself, *Why not? Why do I not share these amazing products and this opportunity with people? Do I not want this anymore? What am I feeling about this? What is going on with my business?*

My background was in science with an emphasis in dental hygiene, not network marketing. I didn't know much about the industry or running a business when I got started. I was a science major not a business major. How I got into the business was interesting.

As a gym rat, I was around a lot of bodybuilders, competitors, and hard-core, physically fit people. One day at a gym back in 2010, I was introduced to an "amazing product" by a personal trainer on steroids. He was the typical short bodybuilder with huge muscles and a little brain. Let's face it; even though all bodybuilders are not like that, that is the stereotype. Well, this guy fit the mold. He said this amazing product would help with muscle recovery. At that time, I was in training to compete and "helping with muscle recovery" was music to my ears. However, I didn't listen carefully to what that guy was trying to tell me. I just figured whatever it was he was talking about had something to do with the steroid line, and I was not willing to have anything to do with those. So, I just kept plugging along focusing on my fitness competition.

I was approached by three other people in a matter of two weeks about the same "amazing product." I took that as some sort of sign, as I was lying awake at night wondering what I could do for a second stream of income. That product was part of a network marketing business that could allow me to earn extra money. I was interested in all-natural products and maintaining my health as well as implementing another stream of income. I made a great income as a hygienist, but I really wanted to sock money away for retirement.

I attended several meetings and talked with several people already in the business to gather information. During the time I was debating whether to pull the plug and start a business with this amazing product, I fell on the ice, almost breaking my left arm. That pushed me over the edge to join that network marketing company as an independent distributor. Falling on the ice caused me to miss a few days of work with a badly bruised elbow. What an eye opener that was—if I could not work as a hygienist, how would I support my family? I was a single mom with two boys.

This business would allow me to earn money as well as help people with their health. Because I was excited about my new adventure and passionate about helping people, my business grew very quickly. I was having a lot of fun, meeting tons of positive, like-minded people, and things were awesome. Network marketing seemed to be easy. I wasn't sure what everyone else was talking about when they said it was hard; as far as I was concerned, it was a piece of cake.

As with everything in my life that was too good to be true, the day came when people thought I was crazy and unprofessional for joining one of "those" companies. I felt I was being judged and started listening to the negative chatter, which caused a negative feeling inside of me, like I was doing something wrong or bad.

I stepped back to take a look at what was going on. I learned I was getting in my own way. I was taking things personally and did not want to share anything with anybody about my business. I was causing the roadblocks that were keeping myself from moving forward. I was believing some of the negative chatter, which triggered old negative feelings of not feeling good enough and not feeling important to resurface. *Wow, who would have thought? I was hesitant to move forward in business because of my insecurities of the past.* That damn past was haunting me again.

Because I had learned those feelings came from thoughts, I had to know what the specific thoughts were, where they were coming from, and why they were surfacing again.

Through building my business and attending events, I met an amazing young woman who was an inspiration to me; I will call her Dawn. She had drive, ambition, determination, and wisdom beyond her years. I learned tons from her about how I could feel good about myself and how I had the potential to be all I wanted to be.

As a result of meditation and questioning from my amazing friend and newly hired life coach, Dawn, I discovered I hadn't felt "good enough" in years. Most of those feelings came from my first boyfriend cheating on me. That'll make you wonder if you're good enough, important, and worthy. But I wanted and needed to know what those thoughts were and the feelings that were being fed. I wanted to know where my low self-esteem and lack of confidence were stemming from.

We kept digging and working deeper. Through more meditation and consulting, I learned I had thoughts that all men are pigs, all men cheat, and men just want women for one thing. I had thoughts of "you can't trust men" in my subconscious mind. Some of those thoughts were fed to me from family and some I drew as my own conclusions from the men in my life. Once I discovered where those thoughts stemmed from, I knew I had to get rid of them. I desperately wanted and needed them gone. I needed to get them out of my head and out of my subconscious mind.

My biological father was an alcoholic, my grandfather sexually abused me, and my first true-love boyfriend as well as other men cheated on me—no wonder I didn't trust men! I justified those negative thoughts I had toward men; however, that didn't make them go away. I realized I had to get those thoughts out of my subconscious mind so I could move forward in business, relationships, and life. Keeping those negative, energy-draining thoughts there kept bringing up those negative, harsh feelings I had of myself of not being good enough, pretty enough, or smart enough and making me feel inadequate.

I made a list of those specific thoughts I had about men, so I could work on releasing the bad, negative, and horrible recollections I had. I learned from Bob Proctor and my life coach how to release those weeds out of the garden in my head.

Again, I felt like I was making great progress. I made the conclusion my business wasn't growing because I was hesitant in approaching people because I didn't feel good enough or didn't feel important. I didn't feel people would want to do business with me or listen to what I had to say. It was amazing to me to make the connection between the thoughts about men in my life and being afraid to move forward in my business. Revealing those limiting beliefs was incredibly healing. I was starting to have faith that I wasn't totally broken; there was hope for me to believe in the good in people.

I looked at my career as a dental hygienist. It had been an amazing career, with great income and no weekend or holiday shifts, and I was never on call. It was intellectually challenging, as I got to educate people about oral health and be creative on why they should floss every day. But I needed something more. I wanted something more out of life. I was not being challenged enough anymore. That was part of the reason I had joined the network marketing group, I needed a challenge. I needed something new. Others thought I was crazy, but in the beginning I did not care. I was passionate about the products, because there was a lot of science behind them and I enjoyed helping people. I also knew I wanted out of the dental field. I wanted to be my own boss and set my own hours. I wanted to be able to take vacations when I wanted. I wanted to wake up when I was done sleeping. I had spent twenty-five years in the dental industry; it was all I knew but I wanted out. Network marketing was a vehicle for me to replace my income and give me the freedom I desired.

Furthering my career as a hygienist wasn't really an option for me, as there was no place else to go unless I wanted to go to dental school, and I knew I didn't want that. Until my new business was my main source of income, I made a commitment to myself to be the best hygienist I could be. My focus would be on my patients, and I would continue to give 100% until I could retire from the dental field.

I have not been confident about many things, if anything, in my life, but I was very confident about my abilities as a hygienist. I was good at cleaning people's teeth and extremely knowledgeable about gum disease and tooth needs. I am kind to my patients and very gentle. People love that and had nothing but good things to say about me.

My next category to evaluate was relationships. *Boy, I know I need help here.* This was going to be tough and rewarding at the same time. I had failed many times in the relationship department on an intimate level, personal level, and professional level. I wanted to evaluate and improve, not just intimate relationships, but ALL relationships: with my significant other, my kids, my siblings, my parents, my friends, my coworkers— with everybody.

I am from a family of divorced parents, who has older siblings who divorced, and I have been married twice. I knew my intimate relationship department needed some attention. I knew this for a while but didn't know how to fix it or change it. I failed over and over. I sought counseling, both individual and couples; I read self-help books and the Bible, but nothing seemed to sink in. I certainly didn't have positive guidance or role models in this area, so I just flew by the seat of my pants.

My mom remarried when I was three, so I was too young to remember any parenting from my biological father. But I am aware of my mom and my stepdad's upbringing. They took care of our basic needs but weren't super loving or caring in a nurturing type of way. They did not show much affection to us kids. I know they did the best they knew, and I truly appreciated the life they provided for me. I have a lot of respect for my mom for taking care of us. Looking back, I wish my parents had known and showed more love, more care, more guidance. We kids never heard the words *I love you, I care for you, you matter*, or *you are important*. We weren't encouraged to do our best; we weren't encouraged to do anything; it was like we all just existed. Some of my older siblings quit school with no consequences, and they got in trouble with no repercussions. It was a free-for-all, and we got to do whatever we wanted. Fortunately, I never got into trouble and didn't rock the boat, but I searched for love. I wanted love and security. I wanted to matter to someone, especially to a man.

I don't mean to be so negative and disrespectful to anyone in my family. This is how I perceived things to be when I was being raised. Like I said, I am grateful for all the material things we had, the roof over our heads, and that we all stayed together. But do I wish things would have been different? Of course.

As I looked back and reflected on the intimate relationships in my life, I discovered I was desperately looking for a man to love me and make me feel important. I wanted to be special to him. I wanted positive love and attention. Because I did not get this from my biological father, I guess I feel I was yearning for what he did not give me. My relationship with my stepdad, whom I call "Pa," wasn't super close, but in his own way I think he loved us kids. After all, he worked hard to take care of our basic needs and wants for the most part. As I grew up, I didn't need a man in my life financially. I could support myself, but I wanted someone in my life. I wanted someone to share my life with. I wanted someone to lift me up, not pull me down. I wanted someone to love who would love me back.

Matt has taught me many things and has qualities I wished I had in myself. He does not take things personally, and he can let things roll right off his back. His skin is pretty thick. He can take things for what they are without reading into the thought too much, which I admire. He is also a straight shooter and will tell you the truth whether you want to hear it or not. I believe sometimes the truth is too harsh and should be filtered. (We continue working on Matt's filter!) He's not very good at sharing his feelings with words, but I know he loves me in his own way. He's very protective and I love that about him. He is a hard worker, takes pride in his work, and never misses time. I am extremely proud of him and admire him for his work ethic.

My family has many faults and many issues, but working hard has always been on the top of our good qualities list. I'm not quite sure where this quality stemmed from, but I have always been super proud of my family for their work ethic. We put our work before family, which is not something necessarily to be proud of, but we work hard, don't miss time, and pay our bills.

I have not been the best mom to my boys, but I gave it my all and continue to do so. My theory as a parent was to do for them what I wished my mom had done for me. I have volunteered at their schools, gone to almost every sporting event, read to them at night, tucked them in bed, and most important of all, I tell them I love them, and I am proud of them as much as possible. Every chance I get I tell my kids I love them, and I tell them they are important to me and they matter! I want my kids to know I will always be here for them, no matter what.

I will cherish the relationship I have with Matthew and Hunter forever. Deep down I feel like my mom had these feelings for me, but they were just never expressed in actions or out loud. I want to make it very clear to my boys how their mama feels about them. I do not want them to wonder. I am so proud of them both.

I realized I have not been the best wife, sister, daughter, aunt, friend, or coworker. I definitely needed to improve the relationship area of my life with everyone I knew. The reassuring thought was the awareness I had for needing improvement. I knew I needed help. I wanted strong, healthy, solid, and secure relationships in my life.

I started with meditation and prayer for the wisdom I needed to grow and nurture the relationships in my life. I knew I was to start with my relationship with me. I needed to get to know me, who I was and what made me tick.

I spent a lot of quiet time meditating about who I was and how I was supposed to get to know me. One of my life coaches I worked with several years ago suggested I just talk to myself as I would talk to a new friend. Ask questions to myself just as I would to someone else. Questions such as what is my favorite color? What is my favorite holiday or meal? What would I like to do before I die?

I dedicated time throughout my day to get to know who I was, what I liked and disliked, what I wanted in my life, and who I wanted to become.

I never stopped reading and learning new things. Another book I read after the accident was *Ask, Listen, and Repeat* by Clay Stevens. It is a book about building lasting relationships through effective communication with people. I learned that I need to be more interested in people rather than try to be interesting, especially when meeting new people. I had a tendency to talk more than listen. This was where I felt I had been selfish: I usually revealed more about myself than I learned about them. My new goal was to find out more about people I met than they found out about me. I needed to ask them more questions than they asked me.

That was a fun game, as I liked asking questions. I have been told by several people in the past that I ask a lot of questions, so I felt this new concept was ironic. For all these years I have been self-conscious about asking too many questions, then I discover I am supposed to be asking more questions. *Hmm, how interesting!* Please note that those times in my life where I heard I asked too many questions it usually came from men who were cheating on me. No wonder THEY thought I asked a lot of questions. They were afraid that if I asked too many questions, they were going to get caught doing wrong. Regardless what those bad, evil, no-good, cheating, lying men thought about my questions, I was going to start a new journey in the question department.

Through counseling I realized there wasn't a perfect relationship out there, but I knew I needed to improve upon what I was looking for in an intimate relationship. I was told I found men like my biological father. I wasn't quite sure what the counselor meant, but that's what I was told. I picked the men who seemed strong yet turned out to be weak, the ones who paid more attention to themselves than to me, and the ones who treated me rotten. I remembered my siblings talking about Adam, my biological father, and from what I gathered he was a no-good deadbeat person who was more interested in his alcohol than his family. Even though I felt the men I dated treated me like crap, I stayed with them and continued trying to make the relationships work. I believed they would come around and love me the way I wanted them to love me—the way I loved them. Not cheat on me because I wasn't cheating on them. I wanted them to treat me the way I treated them. I never wanted to change them. I just wanted them to love me.

I was also told I have codependent tendencies, but I never knew what that meant either. *There must be a book for that.* Fortunately, I recalled a book I had in my own library titled *Codependent No More* by Melody Beattie. I had had that book forever but had never opened it. When I did, it was another eye-opening experience.

I learned that I was codependent, which meant I needed to care for people in order to make myself feel special and important. I would take on somebody's problem and make it my problem. I needed people to rely on me. *Did I focus on their problem so I wouldn't have to deal with my own issues? Or did I just want to help people?* I wasn't sure what the answer was, but I was willing to figure it out. I did not want to be codependent; that thought was not appealing to me.

After extensive journaling and digging deep into my thought process about this codependent concept, I realized what was wrong with me regarding relationships. I knew there was something wrong with my role in any relationship, not just with the men in my life. Well, let's not kid ourselves; there was definitely something wrong with them, but the important fact I discovered here was what my problem was—I was codependent! I never felt it was totally their fault; I knew it took two to make or break a relationship. I knew I had contributed in a bad way to my relationships, but I could never pinpoint my problem.

My old way of thinking went something like this: If he would do "this," I would be happy, or if he would do "that," I would be happy. Or if he just told me he loved me, I would be content and feel secure. I kept journaling and asking myself what I was missing in my behavior regarding relationships, what I wanted out of my relationships—both intimate and casual—and what would make me happy in my relationships. The thoughts discovered from journaling made me evaluate my patterns and my choices.

I realized I should not base my feelings on any circumstance or person. I had been on reactive status, not proactive status. I always let other people's opinion of me set my worth or even my mood for the day. I let other people determine my happiness or sadness. I was dependent upon their approval of me to make me feel good about myself. Once I decided I was important and I was worth it, I was aware that it was up to me, not anyone else, to make me happy. It was up to me to love myself and matter in life regardless of everyone's thoughts and opinions. When I refer to loving myself, I am referring to a respectful sort of way, not an egotistical, self-centered sort of way.

I started telling myself what I wanted to hear from other people. I started treating myself the way I wanted other people to treat me. I was starting a relationship with myself for once. You might think this sounds crazy, and I did, too, at first. But it made me realize I am special. I am an important person.

I still had bad thoughts in my head that needed to be cleared out of there. Of course, I needed some work on releasing all the bad, negative garbage I had in my head.

According to Bob Proctor, our subconscious minds can hold only so many thoughts, both bad and good. We need to release and let go of the ones that are negative and stunting our growth, so we can fill our minds with peaceful and cheerful thoughts. I also learned our subconscious cannot distinguish a real-life event from thoughts that we have had. The thoughts are there whether something really happened to us or it was just fabricated in our minds. *Wow! How crazy is that? My mind cannot tell what's real and what is just a thought.* This was huge for me. Was it possible that most of the negative thoughts in my mind were fabricated and based on events that were not even real? I am not sure if there is scientific proof, but things I recently learned support this theory, and I knew that negative thoughts still had a huge impact on my life.

This led me to learn more about subconscious release techniques, which was so intriguing. I wanted those nasty, toxic thoughts out of my mind once and for all. I reached out to my life coach about releasing techniques and weeding out some of those horrible thoughts in my head. I was now on a new mission.

I wrote down some general issues I wanted to work on first, like thinking positively, being happy, and loving myself. Through a series of questions, we discovered negative thoughts I needed to release. I needed to release thoughts that "I am not good enough" and "I am not important." I would get into a comfortable position in a quiet room and close my eyes repeating after her, "I release all negative thoughts that I am not good enough," "I release all negative thoughts and beliefs that I am not good enough," and "I release all negative emotions that I am not good enough We went through every negative statement releasing all thoughts, beliefs, and emotions associated with them. After spending a few minutes in deep breathing, concentrating on releasing the negative thoughts, I would repeat positive affirmations she stated, such as "I am good enough," "I am happy," and "I am important."

Weeding out the garden of my psyche, getting rid of the ugly weeds, and replacing them with pleasant flowers really seemed to work. Even after the first session I felt like I was on the road to something great and amazing. I was feeling so much better about myself and others around me. I was regaining some of my positive outlook. I was feeling some hope and relief. I realized I needed a lot more work, but I was definitely onto something fabulous.

After some serious journaling and meditation on relationships, I was aware of numerous thoughts, beliefs, and emotions in this department. I compiled a list of my thoughts and beliefs on relationships in order to work on releasing the corrupt thoughts. My list was rather extensive, with some good but mostly bad thoughts. My inventory applied to all relationships. For example, I had concerns that relationships will fail, people are not trustworthy, people don't want to have a relationship with me, all men cheat, men want only one thing, everyone lies, you cannot trust anyone, and people are going to let you down.

I asked myself, *What did I want out of a relationship? How did I want to be treated? What do relationships look like to me? What would make me happy?* Of course, my mind wandered to other questions: *Why did I get in that ATV accident? What did I want out of life? What was my purpose here on Earth.* I knew I would have answers to all these questions someday. I just needed to be patient!

The concept seemed so simple: changing the way you think can build self-esteem, love, and self-respect. You can become more positive and be the person you are supposed to be. No more holding back, no more getting in your own way. If you can get rid of the limiting beliefs that are holding you back, it is very rewarding and beneficial to moving forward. I would say it is simple but not necessarily easy. It takes work, it takes time, and it takes a lot of attention. If you want to do it, you can. I know you can. I believe in you!

I am not saying traditional therapy is bad or wrong, but for me pruning my subconscious mind of negativity and replacing it with positivity made a world of difference. I am sure dealing with my feelings one layer at a time by peeling back that onion would have worked eventually, but this was instantly rewarding. Not that I was expecting instant results—I knew working on myself takes time—but I did want to see progress. Plus, I believed I was going to have better results by focusing on my thoughts versus my feelings.

The Aftermath

"You have a purpose that is so much greater than any mistake or setback you may have made in your past."

—BILLY COX

IT HAS BEEN A LITTLE MORE than four years since the accident, and I feel I have had an amazing life. I am fortunate I get more time here on Earth to live. I do still have issues to work on and I always will. I will never be finished improving my life. My process will be ongoing. I am truly grateful I have learned so much about myself and now have a burning desire to help others. Deep down I am thankful this accident happened; otherwise I wouldn't know my calling or my purpose. I would have missed it. I believe God has a plan for me.

Matt and I ended up getting married and moving to Cheyenne, Wyoming. We continue to have our battles, as any couple does. I still work as a dental hygienist and teach hygiene at Laramie County Community College in Cheyenne. I resumed building a network marketing business, helping people as a life coach, and recently finished my master of science degree with an emphasis in psychology from Grand Canyon University.

My oldest son, Matthew, is now twenty-seven and works for ESPN in Bristol, Connecticut. He has always loved sports and watching TV, especially sports and ESPN, so this is a great fit for him. Who would have ever thought he would land a job getting paid to watch TV? He's probably one of the biggest Denver Bronco fans ever, even in losing seasons. From an early age, he was fascinated by sports—both playing and watching. He played football, baseball, basketball, and soccer, and learned Tae Kwan Do. Soccer became his passion.

I always thought Matthew was ambidextrous, so soccer came easy for him. When playing sports, he predominantly played left-handed even though he writes and eats right-handed. He went to college on a soccer scholarship, majored in journalism, then switched to broadcast. He's got a huge heart with a lot of compassion and is very easy going. He always was happy-go-lucky, even as a toddler. I do remember him getting a little upset in the mornings if his hair wasn't quite right, but other than that, he has a mellow demeanor. At three he took a water bottle to day care to comb his hair after nap time. I'm sure he gets that from his dad. I would also have to say Matthew can be relentless; if he wants something, he doesn't stop until he gets it. I think he gets this from his mama. Matthew is super smart and loves to have fun. I love him a ton and wish him a world of happiness.

My youngest son, Hunter, is twenty-two and a student at San Diego State University studying sports medicine. He, too, loves sports, TV, and weight training. As a child he played football, baseball, lacrosse, golf, basketball, and soccer. Wakeboarding became his passion, and he's awesome at it. He started wakeboarding at the age of four, standing between my legs on the same board. He has advanced nicely and now does amazing tricks. I was so impressed the first time I saw him land a back roll that I was in disbelief. It was so cool! Proud mom moment, for sure. He works as a wakeboard instructor in San Diego where he teaches others his amazing stunts. I think he also is relentless; when he wants something, that is all he talks about and thinks about until he gets it. Hunter is very intelligent, super caring, and compassionate. He has always been determined and is undoubtedly hard on himself, ever since he was young. I think he's a little stubborn, and I'm sure he gets that from me. I love him a ton, too, and encourage him to follow his dreams.

I feel I have been a pretty good mom to my boys, but, of course, looking back, I wished I would have done better. I constantly rehash things I would have done differently. In my opinion, they are great young men, and for that, I am truly grateful. I love them with all my heart, and I'm super proud of them both.

Reaching Out

"If you can help a child, you don't have to spend years repairing an adult."

—JOYCE MEYER

I WOULD LOVE TO SHARE with everyone the concepts that helped me and show others how to become the best they can be. As I said, it is not easy, but it is simple.

I believe the first step to any plan is being aware of the issue. Awareness is key to the process of learning how to love, respect yourself, and get what you want. AWARENESS is essential to any situation. Whatever the issue is you want to change, if you are aware of the problem, you are on the road to recovery. Figure out what things you want to work on or change and make a list. You can break it up into business, personal, career, life, etc. Do not worry about *how* you're going to accomplish your goals; just know what you want and write it down.

Second, remember that your thoughts have created your life. and will continue to create your life, so choose your thoughts carefully. Take a long, hard look at your thoughts. Are your thoughts generally positive or negative? What are your thoughts first thing in the morning? If you can change the way you think, I guarantee you will change your life. You know the old cliché about doing the same thing over and over again then expecting different results? That is downright silly and makes it impossible to ever achieve anything different.

You can reprogram your brain just like you can reprogram your computer. If you do not have the knowledge to seek the results yourself, reach out to someone. Reach out to a therapist, counselor, or life coach to help you get started. Get a game plan and change your life by changing your thoughts once and for all.

It is possible to do it on your own, but I would recommend initially that you get some assistance from a life coach or a counselor. They will help you figure out what your goals are and establish what you want to accomplish. So, knowing what you want must come first. A therapist or life coach will keep you on track, guide you along the way, and support you every step of the way.

Journal about everything! Journal about your feelings, your thoughts, your wants and desires, and even your fears. Write down what you're feeling about each category. Here is where a coach of your choice is super helpful. They can help you connect your feelings to some thoughts that might be hindering your growth or holding you back. This can be incredibly powerful; you will discover things you didn't even know were an issue.

Read, read, read, and listen to CDs or podcasts about loving and respecting yourself, or consume any other motivational material that you find inspirational. Anything positive will help. You need to start retraining your brain to think positive thoughts instead of negative ones. Negative thinking is so automatic, so natural, because it is the way we as a society are, but you have got to change YOU. You need to focus only on you. If you're not getting what you want out of life, turn to YOU, turn within. With help you can discover what is wrong and what you want help with, and find guidance to direct you to a new, better you. Get out of your own way and start being great at being you.

And finally, meditate. This is great for relieving stress and getting relaxed so thoughts can flow freely through your mind. You have to be still to listen; don't try to rush or squeeze in a session. Choose a time when you will not be interrupted or hurried. You can meditate on specific things like being happy or relieving stress or anxiety, or you can keep it general at first and not focus on anything specific. Start small and try three- to five-minute blocks. YouTube has great guided meditations for you to use; these are helpful, as your mind may wander.

For overall wellness you should eat a balanced diet, exercise, and take your supplements.

I wish for you the same things I have learned: love and respect for yourself. Build self-esteem and decide you are worth it, you are important, and you do matter!

Believe in yourself!

Acknowledgments

Although it took several years to final get this book to print, I would like to acknowledge all those that helped me put this masterpiece together.

To my friend, Cherie Robson for giving me the idea of putting my journaled thoughts to pages and write a book. She inspired me to share my story in hopes of helping others.

Polly Letofsky for guiding me through the publishing process. With her expertise and guidance, she put me in touch with all the "write" people. She was extremely motivating and always enthusiastic.

Bobby Haas for the wonderful editing help. He was such a wonderful inspiration and very supportive. He did a fabulous job with ALL the edits.

Victoria Wolf with Wolf Design & Marketing for

the beautiful layout and cover designs, they turned out perfect.

Angela Renkoski for the proof edit. I appreciate her grammatical advice.

My sister Lynn who helped me come up with the title of my book. After she read an early version of the book, we put words together of what my book represented. As a small child I never felt like I fit it anywhere companied with a near death accident the two were tied together, Dying to Belong.

And thank you to all of those that were a part of my life making me who I am today.

About the Author

Diane Mullins has a master's degree in psychology from Grand Canyon University where she learned how to manage, inspire, and motivate people. She has spent most of her life working in private dental offices as a dental hygienist. Diane is a certified health/life coach, which has allowed her to help people with  weight loss, setting goals, and motivation. Now as an author she tells her own story of a tragic accident that taught her things that were crucial to her own wellbeing and that suggested the possibility of helping others in a whole new way.

Diane has coached others on how to get out of their own way by building self-esteem and respecting themselves. She speaks and coaches on subjects she has experienced personally, including the many obstacles of her own she had to overcome.

You can read more by visiting her website
diane2mullins.com

Made in the USA
San Bernardino, CA
19 March 2020

65849163R00110